SEEKERS AND FINDERS
QUAKERS IN HIGH WYCOMBE
1650-2000
A BRIEF HISTORY

Cover picture looking down Crendon Lane c.1900. From High Wycombe as it was, *courtesy of Ivan G. Sparkes and Wycombe Museum.*

Seekers and Finders

QUAKERS IN HIGH WYCOMBE 1650-2000 A BRIEF HISTORY

by
Hugh and Joyce Mellor

William Sessions Limited
York, England

© Hugh and Joyce Mellor 2003

ISBN 1 85072 307 9

Printed in 10½ point Plantin Typeface
from Author's Disk
by Sessions of York
The Ebor Press
York, England

Contents

Chapter			Page
	PREFACE		vi
1.	INTRODUCTION		1
	Appendix	The territory of the medieval borough	7
2.	THE FIRST FEW YEARS		8
	Appendix	Adult members of High Wycombe Meeting 1665	16
3.	BEFORE TOLERATION		17
4.	SETTLING DOWN		24
	Appendices I.	Map showing Meeting House and environs 1877	29
	II.	Sketch plan based on map 1877	30
	III.	Front of first Meeting House	31
	IV.	Interior of first Meeting House	31
	V.	Front door of first Meeting House	32
	VI.	Interior showing screen	32
5.	MIDDLING PEOPLE		33
6.	VIGOUR AND INFLUENCE		39
7.	THE END OF THE BEGINNING		45
	Appendix	Membership of High Wycombe Meeting 1820	53
8.	NEW ROOTS		55
	Appendices I.	Attendance sheet of 'pilot' meeting 1914	63
	II.	High Wycombe Allowed Meeting 1915	64
	III.	Fellowship Meetings	65
9.	HOUSEHUNTING		66
	Appendix	High Wycombe Meeting 1922	71
10.	A MULTITUDE OF CAUSES		72
11.	QUAKER CITIZENSHIP		80
12.	QUAKER COMMUNITY		86
	Appendices I.	Burial Ground 1927	92
	II.	Archives on display in Meeting House	93
	INDEXES		94

Preface

A DECADE OR SO ago we had occasion to give temporary houseroom to certain of the 'archives' of the Quaker meeting at High Wycombe. They included historic documents, such as a copy of a magistrates' committal of Quakers to prison in 1665; illustrations of the first meeting house; and plans of the burial ground. Consequent realisation that the records of High Wycombe Meeting already deposited at the Buckinghamshire Record Office were extensive, probably exceptionally so, dating as they do continuously from the 1650s through to the present day, fired us with enthusiasm sometime to try to give them a wider public. We felt sure that there were various people who would today appreciate knowing about the interesting, lively, amusing and instructive events which have through the years emanated from the relatively small section of the local community which comprises Wycombe Quaker Meeting.

In writing this account we wanted first to provide a history which would be useful to local and other Quakers: but we have aimed also to provide sufficient information about Quakerism itself to make the account intelligible to those who come fresh to the subject; and we have tried to see the events described in the background of their times, and in the life of Wycombe itself, so that those who are interested in local history will also find it of value.

For local history we are immensely indebted to Ashford and Mayes for their two books on the Borough; without them we would have been gravely handicapped, for neither of us are professional historians. In our examination of Quaker records we have much appreciated the help given to us by staff at the Bucks Record Office and of Friends House Library in London. We are also very grateful to Edward Milligan, former librarian at Friends House, for helpful and encouraging comments on the first completed text. Information collected by Cally Trench as part of the preparations for the permanent display of archive material set up at the Meeting House in 2002 has also been valuable.

Finally may we explain, to current members of the Meeting particularly, that we have deliberately not mentioned the names of any who have been part of the life of the Meeting at any time in the period since 1950; with only three exceptions where the account itself would have been gravely lacking without our doing so. The minutes and reports for this period are complete and adequate and the text is based entirely on them. We have not used any anecdotal information – that way we might have met difficulty!

2003

HUGH MELLOR
JOYCE MELLOR

CHAPTER 1

Introduction

QUAKERS FIRST appeared in Wycombe in the mid-1650s. Life in Britain at that time was certainly eventful and life in Wycombe was no exception to this. With an estimated population of 2-3,000 it was one of the larger towns in Buckinghamshire, though slightly smaller than Chesham. It had a flourishing market, predominantly trading in corn: and corn-dealers travelled from London to supply the needs of the fast-expanding capital. In 1604 the market-house was re-built to accommodate this trade.

Market day brought in more diverse buying and selling, and though long-established local traders, such as tailors and hatmakers, were defensive about their trades, men of a wide variety of other occupations settled in Wycombe during this century, such as carpenters, barbers, physicians, and even a tobacco-pipe maker.

The cornmills of Wycombe were already long-established, notably Bridge Mill and Pann Mill (whose wheel is still preserved in situ, nearly opposite the present Friends Meeting House). Early this century papermills were also being built. These were in the Wycombe valley though just outside the Borough boundary. The Wycombe stream was very suitable both for making pulp and for providing power. But the early papermakers were not local men and were resented: and in 1637 a petition against them was sent to the Privy Council, which forced them to close down. This was largely on the grounds that the rags which were the raw material of the trade at that time encouraged pestilence, and further visitations of the plague were feared. The closures however meant that unemployed paperworkers became a heavy burden on the resources of poor relief.

Transport to and from London was by the road following the Wycombe stream via Wooburn and Bourne End, though grain and heavy goods may have joined traffic moving down the Thames at Bourne End or Hedsor. The road to London via Beaconsfield was not built until later in the century. Thus the east end of the town (via "Estyn Town" now Easton Street) was a gate on to "Rye Pasture" at Pann Mill. The northern entrance to the town was at the top of Crendon Lane (now Crendon Street), where a gate led to the track up the hollow way leading to the wasteland of Wycombe Heath. Only the western and southern approaches bore any resemblance to what we know today. (Appendix).

The High Street would probably be recognised by a visitor from the 21st Century because of its width and length – though the street was not yet dominated by the present Guildhall at the western end. From the west the visitor would see the church, though probably be surprised at the small buildings clustering near to it. In the centre the Red Lion Inn would be noted, though it had a normal inn sign (an effigy of the lion, like the one now marking the position, came later). At the east, the White House, a timber framed building not yet stuccoed, would be recognisable, with the brewery which then belonged to it.

Many aspects of life in Wycombe were subject to the responsibility of the Common Council. Its power derived from new charters from Queen Elizabeth in 1598, and James I in 1609. Twelve 'honest and discreet men' had been appointed aldermen and these, with the Mayor and two Bailiffs, formed the Common Council. Thereafter the Council itself elected the Mayor and Bailiffs, and as it controlled the processes by which its own successors were chosen it became a self-perpetuating oligarchy.

Laws were made by the Crown, though Parliament was increasingly exerting its influence against what was regarded as arbitrary government. At local level law was enforced by the Justices of the Peace. Ashford relates that 'Wycombe, under its Common Council, faced with the rest of England, a period of economic difficulty and change, of political and religious upheavals, culminating in the Civil Wars'.[1] Local leaders had a defiant attitude to the authority of both the Crown and the Church. John Hampden, the most famous of all Buckinghamshire opponents of the Crown has his place in history for his refusal to pay ship-money in 1636. Gerard Dobson, appointed vicar of Wycombe in 1629, preached sermons criticizing the official policy of the Church, and with the support of townspeople survived attempts by the Archbishop to remove him.[2]

In 1623 the Common Council was faced with there being 100 unemployed in the Borough, and the demand for relief was overwhelming. The Council became deeply divided about how to respond.

Bad harvests, leading to high prices for wheat, 'the food of the poor', made things worse: and in 1631 plague followed, from which 56 people died. Other illnesses were also more deadly than usual, and local resentment against the Council grew.

To some extent this was overshadowed by the outbreak of the civil war in 1642. Once the fighting began, Wycombe became an outpost of Cromwell's Parliamentary forces against the King's headquarters at Oxford. But even before the war was over, there was a riot one market day in 1649, in which 200 people seized corn from the farmers and had to be suppressed by troops.

In those days politics and religion were closely related to each other. It would therefore be expected that the town was sturdily Parliamentary in the Civil War, and Puritan in church affairs. Puritanism was not a precise term, but within the State church it was applied to a substantial number of people who felt that the bishops were too dictatorial and that there should be more widespread discussion of matters of faith and church government.

Parsons who accepted this could be expected to preach long sermons. They helped to form religious and political beliefs, and amongst their appreciative hearers there were men of influence such as Justices of the Peace. But many of the clergy were less learned or less confident, and 'whilst the sheep looked up to the parochial clergy with considerable interest, they were inadequately fed'.[3]

A system of free-lance clergy, known as 'lecturers', grew up. But this did not satisfy all, and separatist churches began to come into existence at the end of the 16th Century, notably the Anabaptists or Independents, who pressed for the Church's independence from the State. Many of them had to flee for a while to Holland to avoid persecution.

By 1630 the Independents were attracting some of the best elements from the Puritans, and though there are few records about religious groupings in Wycombe at this time it seems likely that Independents were among them. By 1649, according to Braithwaite, with respect to the church as to the monarchy, the old order was gone. Nothing stable had taken its place, though for some the authority of doctrine held sway as never before. But there were others again, the product of the religious travail of the age rather than of any one religious sect, who became known as "Seekers", waiting for further inspiration.

B.A. White summarises nicely the problems of the historian of this period: 'Men's convictions grew from seedling to harvest at breakneck speed in these tumultuous years. This multiplies problems for the historian: a man might be a loyal adherent of his parish church in 1644 and then by turns a Presbyterian, Independent, a Baptist, a seeker and, before the restoration of Charles II in 1660, a Quaker. It is certainly unwise to assume that a man remained a member of that group to which he belonged at the moment when some fragment of evidence brings him to the historian's notice'.[4] At which point it is appropriate to focus on Quakerism, and first on George Fox.

George Fox, founder of Quakerism, was born in 1624, at Fenny Drayton in Leicestershire. In his autobiography, written in 1675, he writes:

'My father's name was Christopher Fox; he was by profession a weaver, an honest man, and there was a Seed of God in him. The neighbours called him "Righteous Christer". My mother was an upright woman; her maiden name was Mary Lago, of the family of the Lagos and of the stock of the martyrs.

'In my very young years I had a gravity and stayedness of mind and spirit not usual in children, insomuch that, when I have seen old men carry themselves lightly and wantonly towards each other, I have had a dislike thereof risen in my heart, and have said within myself, "If ever I come to be a man, surely I should not do so nor be so wanton"'.[5]

By the time he was eleven years old, he had begun to think things out for himself. He was apprenticed to a shoemaker, who also kept sheep and traded in cattle. He learnt to turn out a well-made shoe, and was good with the animals. He was happiest with the sheep, for caring for them at times occasionally gave him time to read and reflect. He grew up into a tall well-built good-looking young man. In his journal Fox describes the first turning-point in his life:

'When I came towards nineteen years of age, I being upon business at a fair, one of my cousins, whose name was Bradford, being a professor and having another professor with him, came to me and asked me to drink part of a jug of beer with them, and I, being thirsty, went in with them, for I loved any that had a sense of good, or that did seek after the Lord. And when we had drunk a glass apiece, they began to drink healths and called for more drink, agreeing together that he that would not drink should pay all. I was grieved that any that made profession of religion should offer to do so. They grieved me very much, never having had such a thing put to me before by any sort of people; wherefore I rose up to be gone, and putting my hand into my pocket I took out a groat and laid it down upon the table before them and said, "If it be so, I'll leave you"'.(6)

Fox left his job, and his home, and for the next three or four years led a wandering life, though at times he returned to Drayton and tried to solve his problems there. But the minister in Drayton who took some interest in him had, according to Elfrida Vipont, 'a Calvinistic gospel full of the dark pessimism which is inevitably attached to a faith which predestines the greater part of humanity to Hell'[7] and this brought him no comfort. He sought advice from many others, but he eventually saw

> 'that to be bred at Oxford or Cambridge was not sufficient to fit a man to be a minister of Christ (and) regarded the priests less, and looked more after the dissenting people. But as I had forsaken all the priests, so I left the separate preachers also, and those called the most experienced people; for I saw there was none among them all that could speak to my condition. And when all my hopes in them and in all men were gone, so that I had nothing outwardly to help me, nor could tell what to do, then, Oh then, I heard a voice which said, "There is one, even Christ Jesus, that can speak to thy condition", and when I heard it my heart did leap for joy'.[8]

Fox came to see that the churches of the day rested on dogma, or the Bible, whereas his zeal was 'in the pure knowledge of God and of Christ alone, without the help of any man, book or writing. For though I read the Scriptures that spoke of Christ and of God, yet I knew him not but by revelation ...'.

Later he wrote of many practical ways in which God's kingdom could be furthered. 'He was to refuse to recognise one code of manners for the rich and another for the poor; he would use the same plain language for all and bare his head before God alone. He was to stand for fair dealing and honesty in trade, temperance in food and drink, justice in the courts, high ideals in education and family life. All these things were to be part of the religious observance of those who gave up their lives to God's guidance. The separation between religion and everyday life was over'.[9]

By 1649 his travels were establishing a new movement of which he was the recognised leader. He had coined the phrase "the Light Within" for the leadings of the Spirit, and for this was arrested in Derby in 1650 and charged with blasphemy for saying that God was to be found in man. He told the magistrates to "tremble at the word of the

Lord", and henceforth the movement was dubbed by one of the magistrates as "the Quakers", a name which has stuck to this day.

Some of the Seekers about the country had become finders at hearing what George Fox had to say, and by 1652 the movement had become quite strong in the north. Quakers there undertook a campaign to the south. They appointed 54 men and 12 women ('The Valiant Sixty') for this purpose, and in due course that brought the movement to Wycombe.

NOTES TO CHAPTER 1
1. L.J. Ashford. *The History of the Borough of High Wycombe*, p.19.
2. Ibid, p.121.
3. C. Hill. *Society and Puritanism in pre-revolutionary England*. Ch.2.
4. B.R. White. *The English Baptists of the 17th Century*, p.31.
5. George Fox. *Journal*, p.1.
6. Ibid, p.2.
7. Elfrida Vipont. *The Story of Quakerism*, p.18.
8. Fox, op.cit., p.11.
9. Vipont, op.cit., p.19.

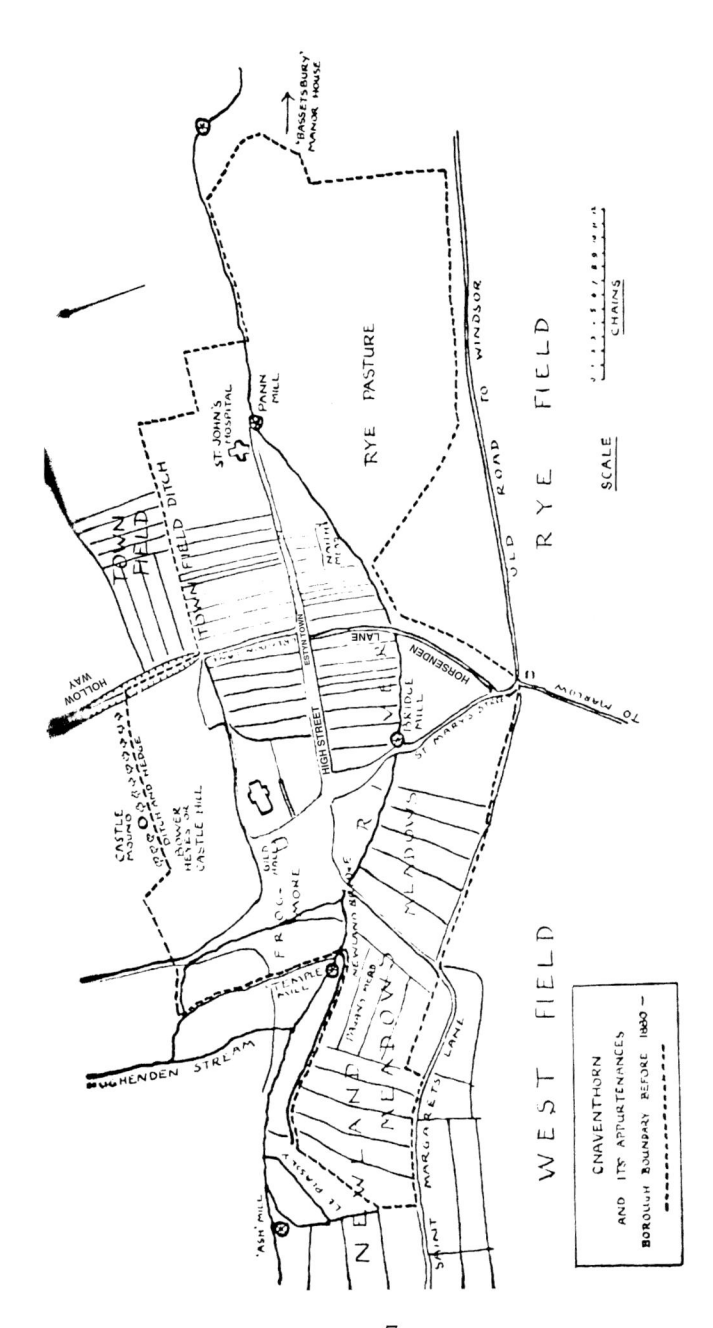

Appendix – The territory of the Medieval Borough (From A History of the Borough of High Wycombe to 1880 by L.J. Ashford, page 27. Published 1960, Routledge & Kegan Paul).
COURTESY OF ROYALTY AND PERMISSION SERVICES

CHAPTER 2

The First Few Years

'AFTER SO LONG a time, whom those friends who first received the Truth in this County are generally gone to rest, the best Account we can recollect concerning the Entrance of Truth here, by whom first published and received is as follows viz:-

In the latter end of the year 1654 Humphrey Smith of ... came to High Wycombe, and having set up his Horse at an Inn and there inquired what Religious People were in that Town, was directed to one Anthony Spire (a Taylor by Trade and one that walked among the People called Independent) to whose house he went. When Humphrey was come, and had some discourse with him, Anthony went forth to Nicholas Noy (a Bodice-maker) and some other of his neighbours, and told them that he had a man of God at his house. Nicholas Noy thereupon and some others went to Anthony Spire's house to see this stranger. After they also had some Conference with him, he desiring to hold a meeting in the Town, they promised him and this was held the next day at the house of one Samuel Guy a woollen draper (where Independents did sometimes use to keep their meetings) and at that meeting Anthony Spire and Nicholas Noy were convinced and received the Truth.

Soon after this came divers other friends at several times to this town of Wiccomb and had meetings there amongst the Independents by which means some others came also to receive the Truth.

And after that they who were convinced tho but five or six in number met together by themselves and sat down to wait upon the Lord in silence; sometimes at the house of Anthony Spire, sometimes at Nicholas Noy's and sometime after at Jeremy Steevens and from thence afterwards at Jno Rannce's'.

This fascinating and detailed account, written it seems in 1676, is unattributable but probably reliable.[1] Records of this period are very few and Quaker records are no exception. The arrival of the stranger, Humphrey Smith, was precisely in the pattern adopted by the campaign to the South of England of 'The Valiant Sixty'. When Quakers entered a new area they seem either to have carried lists of advanced separatists residing there, or immediately to have enquired about them.

Though Humphrey Smith does not appear amongst the names of the sixty he must certainly have been travelling with the blessing of the movement. Braithwaite refers to him as 'a man of rare prophetic gift' who 'was the same age as Fox and came from Herefordshire, where, before joining with Friends, (as Quakers normally described themselves), he had been a preacher of such note that a justice had offered him a maintenance'.[2] This he refused, and later went through a period when he told his congregation that his "mouth was stopped" and he could not preach. It must have been shortly after that that he became a Friend. George Fox mentions him in his journal: Fox was visiting Evesham in 1655 and wrote that he heard 'that the magistrates there had cast several of my friends in prison'; he found that one was 'Humphrey Smith, that had been a priest, but was become a fine minister of Christ'.[3] Smith was also a tractarian par excellence, and though his style of writing is very difficult for readers of today, he seems to have found kindred spirits in Wycombe in 1654.

There is no record of the names of the 'divers friends' who came to the town soon after Humphrey Smith. They would be itinerant Friends, and it is clear that they were important in building up the membership of the meeting, -though there was no formal membership at that time or, indeed, for a long time afterwards. Those who met together were those who were "convinced" and had "received the Truth", and it was as "Friends of Truth" that they were first known.

The anonymous account seems naturally to have picked out the leaders of that time. Meetings were held at their houses. There is no additional information about Anthony Spire the tailor, but the other three names were destined for much mention in future Quaker records. Nicholas Noy the bodice-maker came originally from Bradenham, where in 1648 he married a woman with the remarkable name of Philocrista or Filia-Christi Fish. They settled in High Wycombe.

Jeremiah, probably known as Jeremy, Steevens is the first mentioned member of a family destined to provide membership and support for the Quaker meeting for many generations. It seems from the account that he may not have been amongst the very first members, but he was clearly well-established by 1659, for there is a record of a monthly meeting of Friends from the surrounding area gathering at his house at that date. He was a maltster by trade, and an alderman and common councillor of the town until 1660. He had probably recently married for he and his wife Ann were to have their first child in 1658.

John Rannce, most commonly spelt Raunce, was a physician, who lived in a house in Paul's Row. He also was an alderman until 1660. It may have been a little while before he joined the group, but the autobiography of Thomas Ellwood of Crowell refers to the first meeting Ellwood attended in Wycombe being held at John Raunce's house in 1659. Raunce had a wife Frances and a young family.

Samuel Guy, the fifth name mentioned in the account, does not appear in later Quaker records. He had the house and brewery in the High Street later known as the White House 'where Independents did sometimes use to keep their meetings', and was therefore prepared to let Humphrey Smith hold a meeting there. He became mayor in 1658. But the account rather pointedly does not say that he was "convinced", and it seems likely that he was never counted among Friends. There was a Thomas Lane who, like Jeremy Steevens, hosted a wider gathering in his house in 1659, but otherwise the names of those going to Quaker meetings in Wycombe at this time are not known.

These few names are almost certainly not representative of the Quaker adherents of the day. They are known because they had houses (or outbuildings) large enough to accommodate meetings, so they were almost by definition better off. They were (possibly excepting Anthony Spire) married, and so probably more suitable to receive and sometimes house the itinerant Friends who were then quite numerous. There were no general Quaker records at that time, and official records such as those of the Common Council would only refer to Quakers if they had fallen foul of the authorities.

For the time being there seems to have been little trouble of this sort. These were the days of the Commonwealth, but there were insurrectionary movements, and in the first half of 1655 the Government decided to take strong measures. As Braithwaite describes: 'The course taken was to place the country under the military regime of the Major-Generals, who held office from about November 1655. During the period of arbitrary government which followed, the personality of the Major-Generals and their instructions from Whitehall counted for much more than the law of the land'.[4] The Major-General for Bucks was lenient to Quakers and although in other parts of the country things like refusal to swear loyalty on oath, or doff hats to "betters", or to pay tithes led to severe penalties, this was not so in Wycombe.

It was not that Quakers were inactive. 'Action against oppression, in its various forms, was vital for Quakers', writes Barry Reay. The matter of non-payment of tithes is an illustration. Reay's 1985 history called it 'a guerilla war against the clergy'.[5] Braithwaite in 1911 wrote more precisely: 'Friends refused to pay tithes, as being forced payments for the maintenance of a professional ministry'.[6] Besse in 1753 had elaborated further, on two 'principal points wherein (Friends') Conscientious Nonconformity rendered them obnoxious to the Penalties of the Law:

1. Their Refusal to pay Tithes, which they esteemed a Jewish Ceremony abrogated by the Coming of Christ.
2. Their Refusal to pay Rates or Assessments for building and repairing Houses, or Places, appropriated to the Exercise of such a Worship as they did not approve of.'[7]

However it is described there is no doubt that this was an issue on which Quakers over many generations felt strongly, and by 1656 there were many – elsewhere than in Bucks – who were in prison for non-payment of tithes or rates or for other offences. In Bucks distraint of goods was the usual penalty for non-payment. A country-wide petition was presented to Parliament in 1659 by 15,000 men Friends, and a supplemental paper was shortly afterwards presented by 7,000 women Friends, of whom a number were from Wycombe. The women protested not only about the tithes but also about the sufferings of their families and the arrest of their menfolk. This group was apparently dubbed the "handmaids and daughters of the Lord".

In the civil war most of those who were later to become Quakers had been staunch parliamentarians. They were opposed to the restoration of the monarchy, though far from satisfied with the Protectorate. But Cromwell died in 1658, and in April 1659 republican and sectarian agitation in the army finally brought the Protectorate down, and restored the "Rump" parliament. Quakers were among those who expected great things of the Rump, and pressed their political demands – the abolition of tithes and the state church; religious toleration; law reform. According to Reay, this pressure may have had the opposite effect to what Friends really wanted. 'Quakerism became increasingly viewed with a mixture of alarm and hostility. In other words, hostility towards the Quakers *contributed* to the restoration of the Stuarts'.[8] And in May 1660 the King was restored.

A change was also taking place in Quakerism itself. In June 1659 Fox had been in Mitcham in Surrey to face violent disturbance of meetings there, which he had managed to assuage, and Braithwaite recounts how after this he was "very weak", and 'shortly after went to Reading, where he seems to have lain at the house of Thomas and Ann Curtis for ten weeks in great travail of spirit'. 'This year 1659 is often spoken of as "the year of anarchy". Its distractions and confusions, the internecine struggles of Puritan parties "plucking each other to pieces", the hardening of men's spirits in the growing strife, and the ominous outlook, all these oppressed and well-nigh crushed the spirit of Fox.'[9] But he came out of it, and in doing so seems to have decided that the movement needed firmly to declare that the means by which it promoted its aims would never include violence, (not until that point a matter on which there had been complete unity), and that it needed to pay more attention to its organisation. Historians are agreed that this was a crucial year in Quaker history, when its "second period" began.

To return to the local scene, in 1659 one of the most notable figures in the history of Quakerism in this part of Buckinghamshire made his first visit to Wycombe. He was Thomas Ellwood, of Crowell, nr. Chinnor, Oxon. Bred as a country gentleman he had met Quakers in Chalfont St. Peter and at the age of 20 attended a meeting there. Shortly after, he heard of a meeting at John Raunce's house in Wycombe and slipped quietly into it, and as quietly away afterwards. 'This meeting was like the Clinching of a Nail', he wrote in his autobiography. 'Here began a way cast up before me, for me to walk in.'[10] Thus began a lifetime of service to the Society, and to this part of the county, for he lived near Amersham after marrying, and would come frequently to Wycombe on Quaker business.

It is Ellwood's history that mentions the first impact of the new government on local Friends. In April 1661 he walked to Aylesbury, where he found 60-70 Friends in prison, 'well-nigh all the men-Friends in the County'. This was a result of a Proclamation issued on 10th January, prohibiting meetings of Anabaptists and Quakers and Fifth Monarchy Men, and commanding Justices to tender the Oath of Allegiance to persons brought before them for assembling at such meetings. On the following Sunday Friends met as usual and many were taken. There is a list of the names of the prisoners at Aylesbury, but there are no references to where they came from, and the only one that is certainly from Wycombe is William Sexton. It must surely be the case that there were several who accompanied him from the same area.

In 1662 the Quaker Act was passed. Quakers were liable to punishment if five or more assembled for worship. There were penalties also for any who refused to take an oath, or who maintained 'that the taking of an oath in any case whatsoever (although before a lawful magistrate) is altogether unlawful and contrary to the will of God'. To take it seemed to them to be acceptance that double standards of truth normally prevailed.

Persecution followed, especially in London, but again Wycombe Friends seem to have been untouched, and at the end of the year Charles II intervened, and a Declaration of Indulgence followed. But Wycombe Quakers were not to avoid persecution altogether.

In the First Ledger Book of High Wycombe, for 8 January 1664/5, there is the following entry:

'Memorand: that the eight day of January Anno Domini 1664 (beinge Sabboth day) Samuell Trone, Jeremia Stevens, Nicholas Noy, John Littleboy, John Cock, George Ball, and Joseph Stevens All of this Burrough Labourers and being presented and knowne Quakers having this day Assembled themselves together with divers women at the house of John Raunce in this Burrough under pretence of Religious Worshipp contrary to A Late Act of Parliament, And being brought before us beinge two of his Majesties Justices of the peace for the Burrough aforesayd have acknowledged and confessed the same and thereuppon the sayd several persons were this present day by warrant under our hands and seales committed to the house of Correction in this Burrough there to remayne for the Terme of Three months according to the sayd late Act of Parliament, it being the first tyme that they or either of them have been convicted of the same offence.

Henry Elliott Mayor
Robert Whitton.'

There are three aspects of this committal that will be specially noted. In the first place, all those charged are described as Labourers, whereas it is known that Jeremiah Steevens and Nicholas Noy had other occupations: the conclusion is that the Justices were determined to brand the occasion as one of disciplining a group of roughs. Secondly, the "divers women" were not on this occasion sent to prison. And third, John Raunce, at whose house the meeting took place, was

– for the moment anyway – untouchable, because of his standing in the community.

This adversity is valuable historically in bringing to light a number of names of local Quakers. Some of them were again committed to prison in June 1965. And there was more adversity shortly to come, bringing in another batch of names. Thomas Ellwood was present at the funeral of an Amersham Friend in July 1665 and there were Friends from adjacent parts including a number from Wycombe. Ellwood vividly describes[11] how the body was being carried on Friends' shoulders along the street when a Justice who happened to be in the town rushed upon it 'with Constables and a Rabble of Rude Fellows whom he had gathered together', and struck Thomas Dell who was one of the bearers with his sword. He then threw the coffin to the ground and commanded that those present be apprehended. They were committed to prison in Aylesbury, where they remained for some weeks. Among those from Wycombe were John Raunce, Thomas Lane, William Sexton, Thomas Dell, Joseph Ross and Jeremiah Steevens.

It is now possible to make a list of 24 names of members who were active in the Meeting in 1665 (Appendix). Seventeen of them are men, which is perhaps a misleading proportion, a result of names coming substantially from people committed to prison. Christine Trevett, in her book *Women and Quakerism in the 17th Century* writes:

> 'The opposition remarked on the presence of many women at early Quaker gatherings. The polemicist Richard Baxter asked who made up the Quaker following and it was 'young raw professors and women', he concluded, plus 'ignorant ungrounded people'. (*One sheet Against Quakers*, 1657, p.11). The table of membership in Buckinghamshire, Norwich and Norfolk in 1662, which Vann compiled in *The Social Development of English Quakerism*, (p.82) indicates respectively that in fact 44.9%, 50% and 43.3% of Quakers in those areas were women. The women would have been especially noticed, given the assumptions of the age, and in any case it would have been hard to ignore them. They courted disfavour in the most hallowed spheres, in churches, in the colleges of Oxford and Cambridge and in the courts of law.'[12]

Probably a fairly large proportion of the members in Wycombe were young. Few were known to be married, and those that were had young families. Barry Reay writes of knowing the 'ages of some forty Quakers converted before 1654' and of the first adherents to Quakerism having an average age at conversion of 28. 'Later conversions were slightly older' he adds.[13]

As to social class, the list is not very helpful. Doubts have already been expressed about the description "labourer":and "bodicemaker", "physician", "maltster" and "tailor" are too small a sample for a reliable conclusion to be drawn. Vann's own conclusion is that 'It can be said with assurance that Quakerism at the beginning drew adherents from all classes of society except the very highest and the very lowest', and impressions from what is known about Wycombe Friends would not contradict that.

NOTES TO CHAPTER 2
1. A handwritten copy was found amongst the papers left by an elderly Friend to the Meeting in about 1970.
2. William C. Braithwaite. *The Beginnings of Quakerism*, pp.195-6.
3. George Fox. *Journal*, pp.224-5.
4. Braithwaite. Op.cit., p.447.
5. Barry Reay. *The Quakers and the English Revolution*, p.43.
6. Braithwaite. Op.cit., p.136.
7. Joseph Besse. *Sufferings of Friends*, Chapter 1.
8. Reay. Op.cit., Chapter 5.
9. Braithwaite. Op.cit., p.355.
10. *The History of the Life of Thomas Ellwood*. Ed. S. Graveson, 1906.
11. Ibid.
12. Christine Trevett. *Women and Quakerism in the 17th Century*, p.14.
13. Reay. Op.cit., p.10.

Appendix

Adult Members of High Wycombe Quaker meeting 1665

George Ball	Labourer
John Cock	Labourer
Thomas Dell	
John Kemball	
Elizabeth Kemball	Wife of John
Thomas Lane	
John Littleboy	Labourer
John Mead	
Nicholas Noy	Bodicemaker
Phillicristie Noy	Wife of Nicholas
John Raunce	Practitioner in phissick
Frances Raunce	Wife of John
Joseph Ross	
Sarah Russell	
William Sexton	
Anthony Spire	Tailor
Jeremiah Steevens	Maltster
Ann Steevens	Wife of Jeremiah
Joseph Steevens	Labourer
Sarah Steevens	Wife of Joseph
Samuel Trone	Labourer
Richard Trone	
Nathaniel Wheeler	
Mary Wheeler	Wife of Nathaniel

CHAPTER 3

Before Toleration

THE NEXT TWENTY years were to see the little group of Friends in Wycombe grow in number, organisation and influence, and in no small measure this was due to the leadership that has already been mentioned. John Raunce was the most likely to produce ideas and some fireworks, with steady support and guidance from Jeremy Steevens, and reliable back-up from Nicholas Noy and Thomas Lane. The contribution made by their wives, mostly but not always in the background, must have been invaluable to them and the meeting.

Raunce, Steevens and Lane were imprisoned together in Aylesbury for a month after the fracas at the funeral in Amersham in July 1665, and with them was Thomas Ellwood. He had been close to the Raunces for some years, and when in 1662 he had become seriously ill in London, but was not welcome at his own home at Crowell because of his father's disapproval of his Quakerism, they took care of him. As he wrote in his autobiography, 'I chose to go down to Wiccombe, and to John Rance's House there; both as he was a Physician, and his wife an honest, discreet, and grave Matron, whom I had a very good esteem of, and who (I knew) had a good Regard for me'.

Frances Raunce became one of the first "publishers of Truth" travelling with Jane Waugh, and was at one time said to have been 'preaching to the newly formed Quaker meeting at Turville Heath'.[1] She died in August 1665, almost on the same day John was released from prison. In 1666 Thomas Ellwood was again in prison, this time for 15 weeks, in the House of Correction at Wycombe, and was no doubt visited there by John, but would have been very sad that Frances was no longer there to accompany him.

The year 1666 brought further personal tragedy to John. His nine year old son Thomas died of the plague, of which there had been a resurgence in 1665-6. (Numbers of Quaker deaths from the plague in 1665 were greatest in London, certainly amounting to several hundred). Other Friends in Wycombe died of it in 1666: Joseph Steevens and his five month old daughter Sara, both on the same day; and Richard Trone.

John Raunce married again in 1667, to Elizabeth Brown of Weston Turville. New Quaker commitments were building up for him. As has already been noted, George Fox had earlier concluded that to withstand all the buffetings it was getting the movement needed to establish a strong organisation. His recommendations were that local meetings in an agreed area should each send representatives to a monthly meeting, which should in turn send representatives to a quarterly meeting normally covering the relevant county. Wycombe Friends had therefore to get together with other groups and set up a "Monthly Meeting".

Subjects for consideration at these meetings would begin with relief of the poor, but thereafter other matters would not be specified. In a communication sent to all meetings, Fox recommended visits to 'reprove persons of disorderly life and those who have gone from the Truth, or been married by a priest, or wear their hats when Friends pray', and there is a good deal about marriage. Differences among Friends are to be settled by the arbitration of other Friends, and inquiry is to be made as to any who pay tithes, and so make void 'the testimony and sufferings of all our brethren who have suffered many of them to death'. Sufferings are to be carefully reported to Quarterly Meetings and so to London. Children are to be trained in the fear of the Lord, and burying-grounds provided. Books for registering births, marriages and burials are proposed.

The local meetings (often known as "Particular Meetings") that formed the first Monthly Meeting were as follows: Amersham, Aylesbury, Burnham, Chalfont (=Jordans), Chesham, Chorleywood (Herts), Farnham Royal (=Tiler's), Meadle, Missenden, Owlswick, Rickmansworth (Herts), Watford-with-Flaunden (Herts) , Weston Turville, Wingrave, Wooburn and Wycombe. It was named Upperside Monthly Meeting, to indicate that it covered the part of Bucks in the Chiltern Hills, as opposed to the Vale of Aylesbury. Its first meeting was held in 1669, and it appointed Thomas Ellwood its clerk. (The "clerk", in Quaker terminology, is the person appointed to establish and record, in the meeting itself, the decisions it makes). After moving monthly from one Friend's house to another, it settled at the home of Thomas Ellwood, 'Hunger Hill' in the parish of Coleshill, near Amersham though actually in Herts.

Unfortunately the minutes of Upperside Monthly Meeting at this time do not list those present, let alone where they live, so it is not known who went to them from Wycombe. The Meeting was attended by men only, for although men and women met together for worship, and women later were asked to take particular responsibilities, "business" was assumed to be men's work. References in some of the minutes make it clear that John Raunce, Jeremy Steevens and Nicholas Noy were often there, and it must be significant that the meeting was normally held on the first Wednesday of each month. Only those who were masters of their own working time could normally have managed this; this would have suited the three mentioned, but one wonders whether others would have gone too, had another day been fixed.

In the main the business of the Monthly Meeting during this period was primarily of the nature suggested by Fox. Marriages were given much attention. The basis of a Friends' marriage was the same as it is today. It is well stated in the handbook of Quakerism, *Quaker Faith and Practice*: 'The simple Quaker wedding where the couple, together with their friends, gather in worship is for Friends the most natural setting for the two concerned to make a commitment to each other in the presence of God. With their declaration they take each other freely and equally as life-long partners, committing themselves to joining their lives together in loving companionship, asking God's blessing on their union".[2] At the period now being discussed, a couple who wished to be married in Meeting came in person to the Monthly Meeting and said so; this was called 'proposing an intention of marriage'. The Meeting then usually appointed two or more Friends to discuss the proposal and report back to it for a decision.

The Meeting took much trouble over this procedure, and over the few cases where the report was not to the satisfaction of the Meeting. In 1674 the Meeting advised one couple to wait a month, 'inasmuch as his father refuses as yet to consent', and John Raunce was asked to speak to the latter. Later the Meeting recorded that 'no reasonable answer' could be obtained from him, and that 'he had sworn he would never give his consent': 'which the meeting not judging a reasonable or righteous impediment, expressed their consent that John and Sara might take each other in marriage'.

The Meeting was also concerned that Friends in business should conduct themselves in a responsible way. In 1674 it recorded:

> 'An account being given to friends that Hellen Hawks of Chesham had run out extravagantly in her shop-trade, and thereby contracted great debts, far beyond what her husband and she are any

way able to discharge, whereby reproach and blame is likely to be brought upon the Profession of Truth; the Meeting considering therof, sent a just Reproof to the woman for her Excess, and withal advised her to take especial care, to deal righteously and equally with all her Creditors, and to give them all as full satisfaction, as all her husband and she is worth are able to make'.

In 1675 the Meeting agreed that women should have their own Monthly Meeting. This was in response to advice from George Fox. As Gil Skidmore has written: 'Fox's ideal was that men and women should work together as "helpsmeet" and "co-heirs" in the new gospel order. However he knew that, in the context of his times, it was not enough just to state an ideal, he needed to help Friends by giving them ways to carry it through in practical terms.'

'Fox saw the value of separate women's meetings as two-fold. Firstly, if women met together they might grow in confidence and ability so as to take their full place in the gospel order in a way which would be impossible if they always met with the men. Secondly, Fox was concerned to give women separate responsibility for what he saw as their "natural" sphere of activity. This was to care for the poor, the sick and prisoners, to take charge of the welfare of children and young people, particularly young women, and to investigate and approve proposed marriages'.[3]

This move brought to a head a serious division of opinion in the Meeting. John Raunce and his son-in-law Charles Harris were partisans of a section of the Society headed by John Wilkinson and John Story, which rebelled against the system created by Fox.[4] The points of difference emphasised by Raunce, as summarised by Beatrice Saxon Snell,[5] were:

1. The Separatists saw no service in women's meetings, except for poor relief in large towns, and especially objected to marriages being submitted to them.
2. They objected to the recording of papers of condemnation except on the request of the person condemned. (These were M.M. statements of disapproval of the behaviour of individual Friends).
3. They objected to the attendance of any but specially appointed delegates at business meetings. (Then, as now, any Friend could attend any business meeting).

The controversy led to George Fox attending meetings at Wycombe and Hunger Hill in 1677, to argue the case with John Raunce and others, but no agreement was reached. Raunce later incited young couples to refuse to cooperate with the procedure on marriages, and wrote a scurrilous pamphlet against Thomas Ellwood, who himself published a reply refuting the charges made against him. Raunce set up his own Meeting in about 1682, and the schism continued for some years after that, but the majority of Friends, led by the M.M. clerk, did not support him. In a gesture of sympathy in 1694 the M.M. ordered that a copy of George Fox's *Journal* be presented 'to the Friends of Wycombe meeting, who stand faithful in their testimony against the separation and separate meeting set up there by John Raunce and his party'.

This was a tragic episode in Wycombe Quaker history, not only because of the schism itself, but also because with it went the loss of an important leader of the time, John Raunce, and because it must have broken the close friendship between him and Thomas Ellwood. It would have reduced Quaker numbers at a time when members were needed for support of one another at a difficult period. As to the points of difference themselves, history has seen women taking a completely equal place in every aspect of the Society's work; "papers of condemnation" continued for many years; and the Society has never seriously questioned whether Monthly and Quarterly Meetings should be open to all members. Raunce and his supporters were certainly never going to prevail on points 1 and 3 as referred to above.

On the positive side, what the episode did indicate very clearly was the virtue of Fox's root proposal, the setting up of Monthly Meetings. The opportunity for Friends to discuss matters with the wider group gave them moral support and bound them into a unity which enabled them to work through problems together. The close-knit relationship which these meetings facilitated has lasted to this day.

Persecution in the years 1670-1690 was considerable. The year 1669 had seen the passing of the Second Conventicle Act. It provided for the punishment of any person sixteen years of age or over who was present at a meeting 'under colour of religion in other manner than allowed by the Liturgy', at which there were five or more persons beyond the household. Fines were directed to go in thirds to the King, the poor and the person who informed a Justice of the Peace of such a meeting. The result of the Act was to make informing a profitable trade, and Richard Aris, described by Thomas Ellwood as 'a broken Ironmonger of Wiccomb', was one of three men who tried to benefit by attending Buckinghamshire Meetings to do so. In due course he made a mistake, by laying information against a Thomas Zachary and his wife for attending a meeting at Jordans, when they were in fact in

London at the time. This did not prevent a Justice from fining Zachary £30 and sending him to prison. The Monthly Meeting committed the management of his appeal to Thomas Ellwood, who threw himself into it with enthusiasm and success, and the prosecution was paid for by the Meeting.

In 1689 Mary Sexton was the first woman Friend locally recorded as being imprisoned for attending a meeting. But besides such prosecutions under the Conventicle Acts, Quakers generally were constantly being fined and imprisoned for non-attendance at church, for non-payment of tithes or church rates, and for refusing to take the Oath of Allegiance and other oaths. Thomas Ellwood also wrote up in detail an account of a J.P. 'breaking in with a Party of Horse upon a little Meeting near Woobourn' in July 1683. 'He sent most of the Men, to the number of Twenty-three, whom he found there, to Alesbury Prison, though most of them were poor Men, who lived by their Labour'.

Three months later, before which time one died and one became sick and was released, 'the Twenty-one Prisoners that remained were brought to Tryal; a Jury was found, who brought in a pretended Verdict, that they were Guilty of a Riot for only sitting peaceably together, without Word or Action, and though there was no Proclamation made, nor they required to depart: But one of the Jurymen afterwards did confess he knew not what a riot was; yet the Prisoners were fined a Noble a Piece, and Re-committed to Prison during Life (a hard Sentence) or the King's Pleasure, or until they should pay the said Fines'.[6] Seventeen of them remained prisoners until King James's Proclamation of Pardon in March 1686.

Wooburn is nowadays seen by many as part of High Wycombe, but it is clear that in the 17th Century this was far from the case. Only one (William Sexton) of the names of the men arrested in the incident recounted above appears in the list of members of Wycombe Meeting in 1665. In the lists of Meetings recorded in Monthly Meeting minutes Wooburn appears as a separate meeting in 1673 and 1690, but not in 1713, though there were still some Quaker families there.

There are no records to tell us about numbers attending at Wycombe in 1680, nor indeed for the country as a whole. Rowntree[7] estimated that at this date there were about sixty thousand in Great Britain, and others seem to agree with him that this was when the number peaked. It seems likely that the pattern in Wycombe would be similar, and that there would be about 40 active adult Friends at this date. Two notable new adherents in the period were John Archdale and Thomas Olliffe. Archdale was the grandson of the London merchant who had bought Loakes Manor (later transformed into Wycombe Abbey) in the 1620s. He joined Friends in 1678. Olliffe joined Friends in Aylesbury, where he was a mealman, and in 1688 bought the house and brewery in the High Street, High Wycombe, which had been occupied by Samuel Guy, and is now known as the White House.

Both these men in their separate ways were to play an important part in the next phase of life of the Meeting. By the Toleration Act of May 1689 meetings of Quakers were no longer regarded as "seditious conventicles" threatened by closure, so, as Ashford puts it in a reference to dissenting congregations in Wycombe, 'freed by the Toleration Act from the necessity of holding their services in obscurity, behind the locked door of private houses, they now built themselves chapels'. Friends were equally well placed to respond in the same way: encouraged presumably by the Declaration of Indulgence of 1687 to envisage better things thereafter, John Archdale had in October 1687 granted a lease to them for 40 years of a barn and cottage in Crendon Lane. The land that went with it adjoined that of the property just acquired by Thomas Olliffe.

NOTES TO CHAPTER 3
1. Richard T. Vann. *The Social Development of English Quakerism 1655-1755*, pp.14-15.
2. Chapter 16, section 16.02.
3. *The Friends Quarterly* Vol.27 (April 1993).
4. For a full account of this separation see William C. Braithwaite *The Second Period of Quakerism*, ch.XI.
5. Beatrice Saxon Snell (ed.) *The minute book for the monthly meeting of the Society of Friends for the Upperside of Buckinghamshire* 1669-1690. Buckinghamshire Archaeological Society, 1937.
6. S. Graveson (ed.). *The History of the Life of Thomas Ellwood*. 1906.
7. Quoted by Vann, Op.cit., p.159.

CHAPTER 4

Settling Down

MANY FRIENDS were excommunicated by the established church, and their burials were consequently not permitted in the churchyard, or sometimes only in a separate piece of unconsecrated ground. Friends would not, in any case, have wished to use a priest to conduct a burial service. So, as early as 1663 Friends in Wycombe saw the need for a Quaker burial ground, and leased a piece of land lying at the North End of a close 'called Pannmill Garden near a certain mill called Pannmill' for the term of one thousand years. They seem to have been well ahead of other nearby Meetings in this respect, for it was not until 1682 that Chesham negotiated a 'corner of a meadow' for a Meeting House and burial ground, and Jordans did so in 1688. Quaker burial grounds were acceptable to the authorities, long before Quakers themselves were permitted lawfully to assemble together!

In 1668 Clemence Ming, widow, leased a further piece of land 'being part of an orchard belonging to a missionage'... 'abutting on Townfield on the North and East'. It abutted the original burial ground on the West. In 1694 another two pieces were added by purchase from John Archdale. The land is now a garden accessible from Railway Road.

There is no evidence that Friends in Wycombe intended – as, for example, Chesham and Jordans Meetings did – to build a Meeting House on the same land as the burial ground. After 1687 there was no need, thanks to John Archdale's lease of the barn and cottage in Crendon Lane (Appendix III). Friends may have met there before meetings were legal, but after the Act of Toleration in 1689 plans could be made with confidence to convert the property into a Meeting House.

John Archdale was an unusual person to become a Quaker. Born into the manor of Loakes, whose land extended south from the High Street to what is now Wycombe Abbey, he married young, and travelled to America where he served as a Colonel in the Maine militia. He returned to England in 1665. A little later his wife and a son died. He married again in 1673, and he and his second wife became loyal members of the Church of England. But in 1678 he joined Friends, as did his two older daughters Mary and Anne. He became active in Quaker affairs locally and elsewhere: in 1692, for example, he was appointed with 28 other Friends to lobby Parliament on a Bill to exempt Quakers from oaths. He had acquired interests in the Carolinas, and was often away there, sometimes for some years, and he was appointed Governor in 1694. There he succeeded in having a law passed which freed Quakers from serving in the militia.[1]

John Archdale had more history to make for Quakerism. In 1698 he was nominated to stand for Parliament by churchmen opposed to the dominant Thomas Wharton, and he was elected. He told the House of Commons that he had been chosen, despite being a Quaker, by the majority of "the Church of England party" without his own seeking. He was the first Quaker to be elected to the House, but because of his religious convictions was not prepared to take the oath. He was not therefore allowed to sit, and a writ for a new election was issued early in the following year.[2]

Friends were probably not finding it easy to have to hold all their meetings in private houses. They would meet at least twice a week, and at that time there might have been thirty persons present. John Raunce had started his own breakaway meeting, so his house was no longer available. The only suitable alternative accommodation would probably have been in the Steevens or Lane households. John Archdale may occasionally have provided a room at Loakes park, but his long absences from home must often have ruled this out. So the attraction of having a Quaker Meeting House must have been great.

It seems likely that Archdale realised that the forty year lease of the old barn made in 1687 could be improved on now that it was to become a long-term home for the Meeting; and before he went off to the Carolinas in 1693 he extended it to ninety nine years. (In 1726 his heirs, for sixty pounds, released the Meeting House buildings and land with them in perpetuity).

The map and sketch plan (Appendixes I and II) show the property as it appeared in 1877. It stood on land up Crendon Street from where, in 2002, number 21A is shown. The double hatched area, it is clear from available elevations, must have been added at some time to the original barn.

Crendon Lane ran north from the High Street, the eastern boundary being identical with that of today's Crendon Street. It was extremely narrow, the carriageway being ten feet across, and had footpaths about four feet wide on either side at the part where the barn stood. The property was entered through a door opening on to the street, leading into a passage which gave access to the barn. The door itself was removed in the 1930s to become the front door of Bassetsbury Manor (Appendix V).

The Meeting Room was forty three feet in length, and twenty five feet in width, enough (according to the Ordnance Survey) to seat 200 people, though probably never required to do so. The plan shows four windows and the sketch of the front elevation (Appendix III) makes it plain that these were well above the lane, so worship would not have been disturbed by looking out! The interior appearance of the Meeting Room, as sketched by Francis Colmer in 1924 (Appendix IV), shows the door from the passage, with a bench on the left which is still in use in the present Meeting House.

The 1687 lease had been conditional on Friends first making a habitable cottage out of part of the premises, and this they did. There are no records of what alterations the Meeting made to the premises after that. It seems likely that they would not have hurried to do more than necessary repairs at first, and perhaps given the room a ceiling: and no doubt stoves would have to be installed for heating. There was no demand for many years for Monthly Meeting to gather anywhere but at Thomas Ellwood's house at Hunger Hill, near Amersham, and therefore there was presumably no demand for separate rooms for concurrent men's and women's business meetings. A moveable screen was erected at some time (Appendix VI), probably before the first Monthly Meeting which did take place in Wycombe in 1728. Similar screens may be seen even now at Chesham, Amersham and Jordans Meeting Houses.

It was the recollection of one elderly Friend[3] in 1990 that in the 1920s access to the Meeting House was *through* the tunnel and in at the back through a door on the left; and the north facing wall on the extension at that point would certainly have made for convenient alternative access if that was called for. There would be good reason in that the passage from the road was quite narrow, and entrance to the Meeting Room through a door from it might have proved difficult with fairly large numbers of people. The extension probably took place in 1794, when Wycombe Friends referred plans 'for altering this Meeting

House for the accommodation of holding the Monthly and Quarterly Meetings' to the Monthly Meeting, and requested its assistance.

The MM appointed six Friends to assist, and approved an expenditure of £160, of which Wycombe Friends had raised £103. The extension could have provided an entrance hall and one or two other small rooms:the estimates included 'plumbers work' but it would be too optimistic to hope that this included the provision of one of the water closets which had been invented towards the end of the century: sewers were woefully inadequate and the town did not have a public water supply until the 1870s. The cottage had a well, and this presumably was shared with the Meeting House in early years.

The plan also shows a gate from the grounds into the brewery (now White House) garden, the house itself being entered from the High Street some seventy yards to the south. Thomas Olliffe bought this property in 1688, though it seems he may not have moved house from Aylesbury until some years later. Indeed the official record of the 'Sufferings of Friends' states that 'Thomas Olliffe of Aylesbury (our underlining) was imprisoned from 1693 to 1695 for non-payment of tithes[4] – the last Quaker in fact, in this area, to be as harshly treated for the offence. Olliffe, whether from Aylesbury or from Wycombe, proved to be a great asset to the Monthly Meeting over many years. He was a partner in a mill with Jeremiah Steevens from the early years of the 18th Century until the 1720s. There are all sorts of unofficial indications that local Friends benefitted from his neighbourliness, using the connecting gate between the properties. He died in 1726, and his son, also Thomas, appears often in the Monthly Meeting minutes from 1728 on.

From quite early in the 18th Century Friends took intense interest in the personal conduct and morality of their members. Wycombe Friends were concerned 'to reprove and exhort those who through unwatchfulness have been drawn into the snares of the Evil One'; and at 'a disposition in some of our youth to be drawn into vanity'. Friends were disowned, for example, for 'misconduct in business' or 'unchaste, loose, anti-christian conduct'. They set up barriers against the contamination of 'the world'.

Widely within the Society at this time 'withdrawal from the world' became associated with a change in the nature of Quaker worship, in which not only did it consist of an openness of the spirit to God, but also of an attempt to obliterate any use of intellectual faculties. This led to the silence of their meetings rarely being broken by the spoken word. It is likely that this 'Quietism' also prevailed in Wycombe.

Friends however were not wholly withdrawn. They maintained their protest against tithes, suffering extensive distraint of goods in the process: and there were some who were sufficiently of the world to be prepared to be burgesses, though this required little but a passive role. This was a period too in which considerable efforts were made to help members or their families who needed employment or were in other trouble.

A somewhat challenging quotation from G.M. Trevelyan may suitably end this chapter.

'In the reigns of William and Anne, the Friends had become numerically one of the most powerful of the English sects. They settled down in the Eighteenth Century as a highly respectable and rather exclusive 'connection', not seeking to proselytize any more, but possessing their own souls and guiding their own lives by a light that was indeed partly the 'inner light' in each man or woman, but was also a tradition and a set of spiritual rules of extraordinary potency, handed on from father to son and mother to daughter in the families of the Friends.

'To maintain the Christian quality in the world of business and of domestic life, and to maintain it without pretension or hypocrisy, was the great achievement of these extraordinary people. England may well be proud of having produced and perpetuated them. The Puritan pot had boiled over, with much heat and fury; when it had cooled and been poured away, this precious sediment was left at the bottom.'[5]

Records of Friends in Wycombe to 1740 seem to support Trevelyan's assessment of the situation. But, as he recognises in later chapters of his history, this was a period of transition, and there was much more to come.

NOTES TO CHAPTER 4
1. Kenneth L. Carroll. *John Archdale's Quakerism*. Journal of the Friends Historical Society, Vol. 57, No.2.
2. L.J. Ashford. *The History of the Borough of High Wycombe*.
3. Peter North, member of High Wycombe Meeting at that time.
4. *Great Book of Sufferings*, Vol. VII.
5. G.M. Trevelyan. *English Social History*.

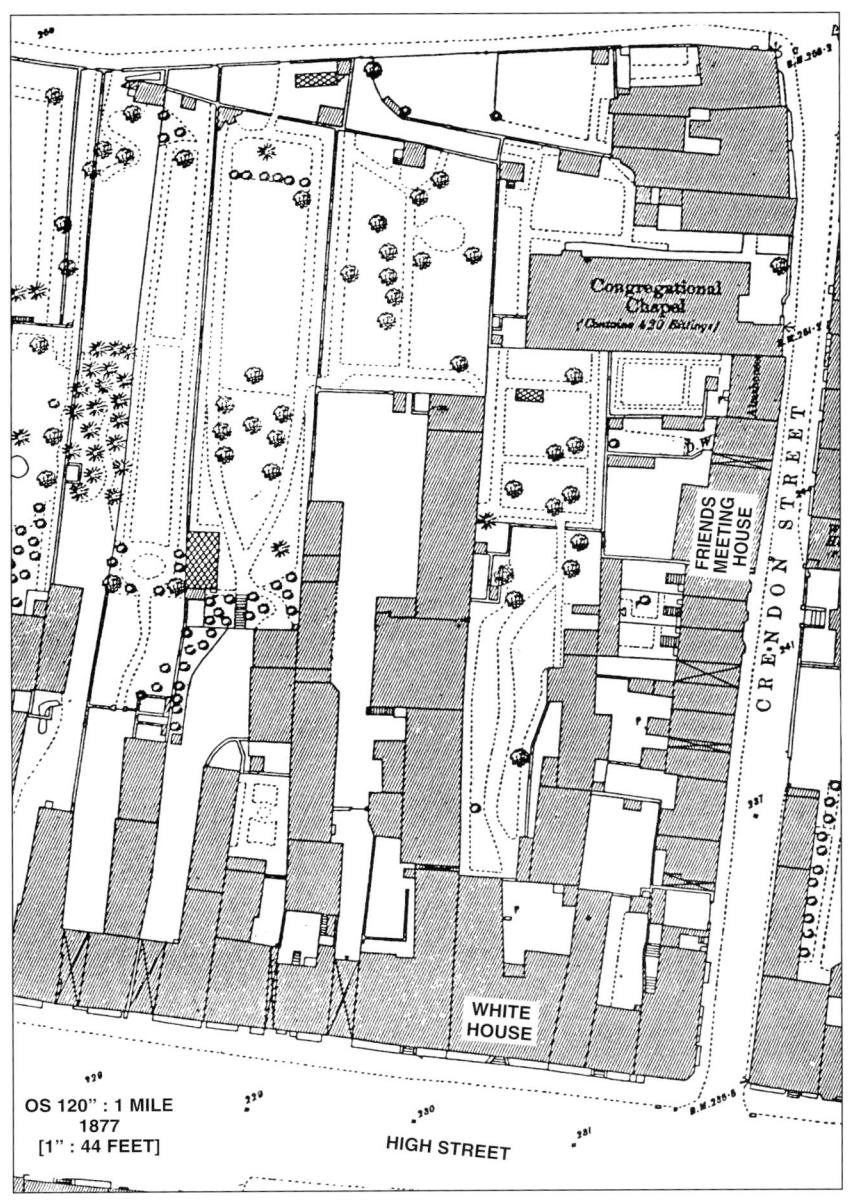

Appendix I – O.S. 120" to 1 mile 1877.
COURTESY OF BUCKINGHAMSHIRE RECORD OFFICE

29

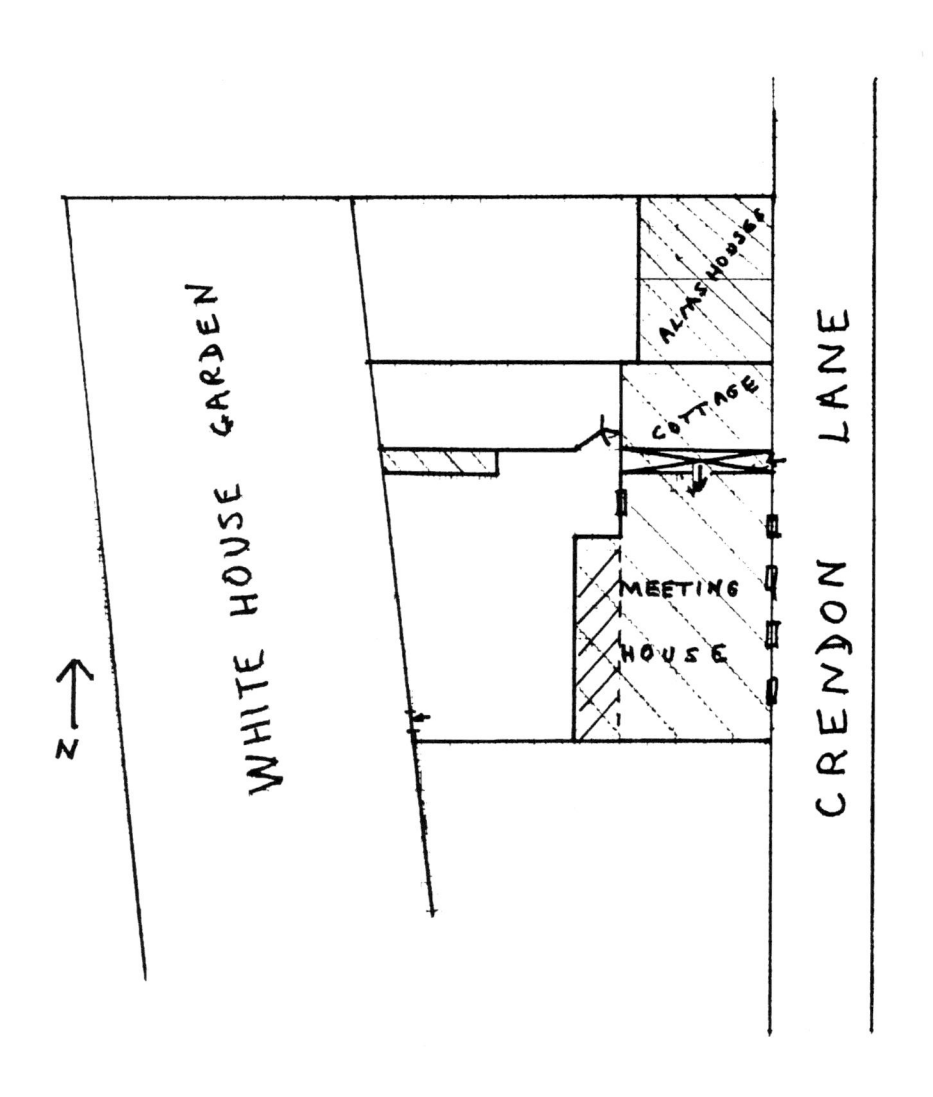

*Appendix II – Sketch plan based on map of 1877.
Scale approx. 1cm : 10 feet.*

Appendix III – Front of first Meeting House. Drawing by Francis Colmer.
COURTESY OF BUCKINGHAMSHIRE COUNTY MUSEUM

Appendix IV – Interior of first Meeting House. Drawing by Francis Colmer.
COURTESY OF BUCKINGHAMSHIRE COUNTY MUSEUM

Appendix V – Bassetsbury Manor front door. Door of old Meeting House in Crendon Street.
PHOTO: CALLY TRENCH

Appendix VI – Screen in first Meeting House. Drawing by unknown artist.
COURTESY OF HIGH WYCOMBE QUAKER MEETING

CHAPTER 5

Middling People

ASHFORD DESCRIBES the eighteenth-century market town of Wycombe as 'an attractive place, beautifully situated: busy, prosperous and privileged; its appearance praised by every topographer'.[1] New houses had been built along the western boundary of the borough, overlooking a central green in Frogmoor, which had a lake, and 'grass, walks and trees'. At the eastern entrance to the town the narrow bottleneck was enlarged by the Trustees of the Beaconsfield-Stokenchurch Turnpike Trust in 1767, by pulling down part of the grammar school, and thereafter the London road grew in importance and brought much prosperity to Wycombe. Roads generally in Britain were bad, though improving from 1740, and river traffic was extensive, supplemented ere long by the development of canals.

At the end of the previous century thirty eight different occupations had been represented in the burial records of the ninety inhabitants of the borough; and a hundred years later the trades practised were equally varied. At the middle of the 18th Century the casual labourer's wage was 1s.2d (6p) per day, and by 1780 it was 1s.6d (8p). In the country generally, due to advances in agriculture, there was more food available. Death rates were smaller, due to advances in medicine. The poor however were harshly treated, as workhouses were established in mid-century, and relief was denied to any who refused to enter them: all classes of the destitute were confined under conditions of acute shame and degradation.

It is against this background that Quaker life in 18th Century Wycombe has to be described. The more detailed information covering this period has to come from the minutes of the Monthly Meetings (MMs), for there are no extant records of the local ("Particular") Meetings (PMs) for the period up to 1799. Men's MMs met in various places in turn. Each PM sent one or two representatives. Although other men Friends could also attend, the impression from the minutes is that few did so, and that representatives from each PM were drawn from a small core of their members. They would be limited perhaps to those who could spare the time from their businesses, were better off, and were well placed to travel. Isabel Grubb has described 18th Century travel vividly:

> 'In spite of the difficulties, dangers, and slowness of travel, Friends moved about freely, sometimes by coach or canal boat, or, if able to afford it, by chaise or on horseback. Poorer Friends went on foot. Sometimes men and women rode single, sometimes the woman would ride on a pillion either behind a man Friend or the servant who went with them to bring back the horses. A swift horse might be the means of saving its master from robbery or even death, for the roads were the haunt of highwaymen especially in lonely parts.'(2)

From 1675 there had been Women's Monthly Meetings, held on the same day, close by where the men were meeting, and in view of the hazards of travelling it is not surprising to find that many of those who attended were the wives of active members of the Men's MM.

Records of the composition of Meetings are exasperatingly lacking. Minutes do not include numbers of people present on any occasion, or provide figures of membership at any time. There is just one "glimpse" into the sizes of local Meetings in the 1770s, when the MM had to ask PMs how many copies of the printed Epistle from the Yearly Meeting they wanted, and recorded numbers as follows for Wycombe: 1773 16, 1775 24, 1776 30, 1777 18. These were larger numbers than for any other Meeting, Chesham and Jordans being the next in size at 12-13 each. These figures probably represent the numbers of families with one or more active members, and it seems that numbers were down on those of 1740. This is consistent with Quaker official estimates of membership in Britain generally.

This was a period in which membership was proving a difficult issue for the MM. From early days Quakers were simply people who attended Quaker meetings: if they were men, their families were assumed also to be adherents, and in the early days this was probably correct: but in general it was not until the later eighteenth century that there was any systematic effort at listing who were in fact members. When formal membership was instituted in 1737, (primarily to assist with pastoral care), all members of families were put on such list as there was, and as John Punshon has pointed out, 'there grew up a class of habitual birthright Quakers, distinguished by adherence rather than commitment. It has been estimated from Yearly Meeting records that there were three disownments for every two convincements, and that by 1750 the overwhelming majority of Friends, perhaps eighty per cent, were birthright members'.[3]

The consequence, certainly for Upperside MM, was that a great deal of time was spent in considering and responding to reports of Friends acting in ways offensive to Friends' principles. In the period 1762-1785, 15 members were disowned for misconduct or total lack of interest, and 11 others for "marrying out". Some of these would be from Wycombe. The MM was also concerned at the number of nominal Friends, who were not necessarily letting down "the Truth" but who had ceased to attend Meetings.

Most frequent among the misdemeanours cited are drunkenness and being in debt. The former is unsurprising for the time, when, as Trevelyan relates, 'drunkenness was the acknowledged national vice of Englishmen of all classes, though women were not accused of it. A movement for total abstinence was out of the question, in days before tea or coffee could be obtained in every home and when the supply of drinking water was often impure'.[4]

Disownment as result of "marrying out" has been held in Quaker circles to be responsible for the sharp decline in numbers of members in the period 1750 onwards, though Punshon writes in this connection that it is tempting 'to take official pronouncments with a pinch of salt'.[5] The records of Upperside MM would support such scepticism: 11 disownments for this reason in 24 years cannot in themselves have been disastrous. Nor did all such disownments lead to long-term loss of support: Joseph Steevens, for example, was disowned for marrying Elizabeth Hawgood in 1781; they applied unsuccessfully for membership in 1787, but were accepted, with their four children, in 1792. They became active members, Elizabeth becoming a greatly respected elder in 1799.

Cases could also be cited of Friends who were disowned for their financial misdemeanours coming back into the fold. And there is encouragement to be had in the reference in the Dictionary of Quaker Biography at Friends House Library to Joseph Green, who moved to High Wycombe in 1779:

> 'Joseph Green inherited a moderate fortune from both his parents, but his financial resources were not equal to the demands he made upon them. Although nominally a Quaker and hospitably entertaining Quaker ministers visiting the neighbourhood, his style of life, his card playing, conviviality and fondness for field sports were

not such as to commend him to plain Friends. His wife (Mary) at that time was no less attracted by a gay life and hunted the countryside in a scarlet riding habit. He died on 31 July 1786 at the early age of thirty eight, leaving his wife £2, 000. Her character altogether changed, she became serious, donned plain Quaker dress and brought up her family of three daughters and two sons with a strict regard for the beliefs and principles of the Society. In later life she became a valued Quaker minister'.

Information about the occupations of Wycombe Friends during the period is as seriously lacking as it is about numbers. It was possible to add occupations only to 22 names on the authors' database for 1701-1750, and 10 for 1751-1798. The list for the first half century was as follows:

1 miller	1 schoolmaster	1 chandler
6 maltsters	2 salesmen	1 bodicemaker
3 mealmen	2 drapers	1 baker
	1 milliner	1 carpenter
	1 shopkeeper	1 bricklayer

For the second half century there were 3 gentlemen,[6] 6 mealmen, 1 grocer, 1 ironmonger, 1 draper and 1 bricklayer. These figures are of course no bases for very firm conclusions, but it seems reasonable to say that whereas in the early period people from professional, merchant, artisan and service classes were becoming Friends, later the merchant and the "gentleman" seem to prevail. Writing in 1761, William Beckford considered the 'middling people of England' to consist of "the manufacturer, the yeoman, the merchant, the country gentleman". It seems that Wycombe Friends were becoming "middling people".

In passing it is also of interest to note that of the Friends most often representing Wycombe at Monthly Meeting during the period 1762-1785 whose occupations are known, three were mealmen or maltsters, one was a gentleman, and one an ironmonger. These representatives were, as surmised earlier, men of independence and comfortable means.

It is agreed by historians that in England in the second half of the 18th Century Friends were achieving eminence through science, medicine, trade and banking: in Wycombe such worldly success was particularly evidenced in the corn trade.

From earliest times Yearly Meeting addressed "Queries" to Quarterly Meetings, and they to Monthly Meetings, as to the religious principles to which Friends were expected to conform. MMs likewise addressed queries to PMs, and from replies to these latter it is possible from time to time to get some idea of a PM's "condition". It cannot be said that Wycombe Friends in the second half of the century were complacent about the state of their meeting, but in 1743 they had recorded two matters of positive satisfaction. The first was that 'the necessities of the Poor among us are duly supplied'. In the decades that followed MM spent a good deal of time on the care of Quaker poor. Their minutes authorise the treasurer to make payments to various individuals; record an endeavour to assist a member who could not get employment; show their concern for one who 'has been for some time in hospital but now removed and in want of assistance'; organise fund-raising for the new Quaker school at Ackworth; and hence, authorise payments 'on account of Wm. Jackson's Schooling at Ackworth' in 1787.

The second matter for positive report by Wycombe Friends in 1743 was that 'our Testimony against payment of Church Rates, so called, Tithes etc. is pretty generally kept up'. The Great Book of Sufferings at Friends House, London makes it clear that Friends were subject to much hostility over non-payment of tithes until the end of the 17th Century, and – as indicated in chapter 4 – Thomas Olliffe was imprisoned for two years on this account. Thereafter the Book shows a record of about 12 households each year from Wycombe being subject to distraint of goods, until in 1760 the average dropped to 6. The numbers rose a little at the end of the century, but even allowing for reduction of membership the impression is left of a lessening of hostilities between Friends and the authorities from this date.

This is borne out by examination of what the distraints imposed were. In 1751, for example, 5s.10d was taken from a carpenter, whose earnings at that time would have been about 2s.0d per day. The sum demanded for the tithe itself was 3s.9d, the rest being costs, so the actual "tithe" was considerably less than half a week's earnings, equivalent to an annual tax of 1%. It is the view of one historian, Eric Evans, that 'many Quakers did in fact permit tithe owners to enter their fields and take the tenth. If tithe owners ignored the legal nicety of waiting to be informed of a crop's readiness for tithing, the Quaker's pacific beliefs did not permit him to restrain the titheman in his work. A "modus vivendi" was thus established'.[7] Eric Evans does not relate whether or how this sort of understanding applied to a carpenter who had no field.

Yearly Meeting was not happy with the situation, and a MM minute in 1772 referred to 'several members which are not clearly respecting our Testimony against the payment of Tithes etc. 'and called for a report, but there is no indication of further action. It seems likely, as Evans goes on to conclude, that tithing obligations became 'no more than a constant and nagging ulcer of discontent'.[8]

The impression of Quakers in Wycombe towards the end of the 18th Century is that they were a fairly prosperous group, watchful over their members' welfare and good conduct, no longer aggressive in their testimonies, and not being gravely provoked by state or society to become so. Their support for any wider Quaker witness, such as the campaign for the abolition of slavery, was evidenced only through their support, through MM and QM, for Yearly Meeting activity on such issues. The end of the century, however, was to see changes in attitudes.

NOTES TO CHAPTER 5
1. L.J. Ashford. *The History of the Borough of High Wycombe*, p.200.
2. Isabel Grubb. *Quakerism and home life: an eighteenth century study*. In *Children of Light*, ed. Howard Brinton, 1938.
3. John Punshon. *Portrait in Grey. A short history of the Quakers*, p.135.
4. G.M. Trevelyan. *English Social History*, p.314.
5. Ibid, p.151.
6. Defined in the *Shorter Oxford English Dictionary* as 'a man of superior position in society; often of money and/or leisure'.
7. Eric J. Evans. *The contentious tithe*, p.59.
8. Ibid, p.62.

CHAPTER 6

Vigour and influence

FROM TIME TO time in the Monthly Meeting minutes of the 1780s reference was made to Adey Bellamy, generally in connection with a service he was able to undertake for it in London, such as finding a ship to convey a message to a Monthly Meeting in North America. He was it seems quite well known within the compass of the Upperside MM, perhaps because he visited frequently and attended Meeting for Worship in Wycombe.

Adey Bellamy was born in Suffolk in 1739, and at about the age of eleven he was placed with a relative in London and was subsequently apprenticed to him. He became a cutler and at his marriage in 1774 was described as "a citizen of London", where he lived in The Poultry. He continued in trade in London for many years, where he was said to have conducted himself 'with integrity and uprightness, but not allowing his business to hinder him from being an active member of the Society'.[1] His wife Martha died in 1786, and he was married again, to Judith Whiting, in 1789. He retired from business and they took up residence in High Wycombe, where they leased a house in Easton Street from the Corporation.

Upperside MM was delighted to have him. They accepted his membership in November 1789 and immediately appointed him to represent them at Quarterly Meeting. In July 1790 he became an elder, and for nearly twenty years he was amongst the most active of local Friends. His wife was also active in the Society, but died in 1801 at the age of only 50.

On arrival in Wycombe Adey Bellamy joined the small band of Wycombe Friends who faithfully resisted the payment of tithes. In 1791 his name appears in the list of those who suffered distraints for non-payment of 'Church rates so called' (as the Quaker records refer to them). Others regularly in the list were James Hargr(e)ave, Mary Steevens and sisters, Edward Fage, George Orger, John Walduck and

Thomas Edmonds. But demands were to come from elsewhere than the Church. In February 1793 France declared war on Britain, and before long Britain became an armed camp, with about one sixth of the adult male population under arms at any stage of the period until the war was over in 1815: a troop was established in Wycombe, and in 1799 the Royal Military College organised the training of army officers from a building in the High Street next to the Red Lion. This may have brought 'a considerable impulse to the gaiety and social intercourse of the place', as one report had it, but military preparations had to be paid for, and new demands were made on the population for this purpose.

In 1793 the Militia Rate was imposed; in 1795 there was the Sailors Rate, to raise men for the navy; later there was the "Fine" made under the Cavalry Act, about which in 1797 the Yearly Meeting minuted that it was 'concerned to find that it is in any degree necessary to declare, that the said Fine, and all other Fines, imposed in lieu of military service, let the application be what it may, cannot be actively complied with by Friends, consistently with our principles'. In response to all these demands, the same body of local Friends refused to comply, and distraints were made upon them – including even on "Mary Steevens and sisters". The tax collector had no difficulty with accepting equality of the sexes!

Further trouble could have arisen in the period which followed. In 1798 the Sheriff of the County compiled what became known as the Buckinghamshire Posse Comitatus, so that men who could if necessary be recruited to an army against Napoleon were known. It was 'a Register of the Names and Occupations of all persons residing within the said Borough not engaging in any military capacity between the ages of Fifteen and Sixty Years'. The instructions for the return included 'distinguishing those who are Clergymen, Licensed Teachers of any separate Congregations, Quakers ...', and Quakers listed for Wycombe were Adey Bellamy, George Orger, Samuel Edmonds, Thomas Edmonds and Thomas Orger. The fact that the returns also included information such as that Samuel Edmonds had a water mill which ground 10 loads per week, or that Thomas Edmonds had one horse and one cart, implied that the possibility of commandeering other resources than personnel suitable for the prosecution of the war was in mind.

As it turned out, in 1802 Friends were exempted from military service, and being subject to frequent distraints on property was the extent of the trouble between them and the authorities over their attitude to war. The Yearly Meeting "Meeting for Sufferings" scrutinized all the Militia Acts during the war, and advised Friends about them, and also turned their attention to relief work called for by the effects of war, for example in Germany or in Greece (for which they set up their own relief fund and sent doctors and a dispensary).

Adey Bellamy was active in a quite different direction also. Public affairs in Wycombe had since 1754 been under the control of Lord Shelborne (later Marquis of Lansdowne) of Loakes Manor. As an Alderman of Wycombe he used his influence to introduce his supporters into the Common Council and so to manipulate the appointment of burgesses (who were the electorate of the day) as to secure the return of his friends, unopposed, to two seats in Parliament. But in 1790, for the first time for 100 years, the family of the Lord of the Manor of West Wycombe put up a competing candidate and there was a poll. The voting showed that there was substantial opposition to Lord Lansdowne's candidates from the burgesses of the town. Ashford describes the next move:

'It had been a near thing, and Lord Lansdowne was jolted into action. In the following January both he and his son, who was also an Alderman of Wycombe by this time, attended a meeting of the Common Council from which the three rebel Aldermen were absent. Fifteen new burgesses were then elected, including six citizens of London, five country gentlemen and four Wycombe men, so increasing the balance of 'foreign' influence against the rebellious local burgesses'.[2]

At the by-election of 1794 the Lansdowne candidate was as result in no danger. But there was turmoil in the town, and Adey Bellamy decided to put forward a plan 'to prevent strife and contention among the inhabitants'. The number of burgesses was to be limited to sixty; no new 'foreign burgesses' were to be elected; no new burgess was to be proposed unless he had lived for twelve months in or adjacent to the borough and was 'rated at £8 a year at least to the Poor Rate'. It says much for Bellamy's political shrewdness and the influence that, it seems, he exerted, that the plan was adopted, with the approval even of Lord Lansdowne. It was carried out for nine years, by which time circumstances had changed considerably, and in 1803 it was dropped. Though its effects could not be called permanent, some of its provisions, Ashford points out, anticipated very nearly the provisions of the Reform Act of 1832.

Travelling ministers played a large part in early Quakerism. They 'provided the means whereby a unity of practice and profession was maintained wherever Friends settled'.[3] But only rarely had Friends in Upperside MM during the latter half of the 18th Century shown a concern to be part of this exercise. However, well before Adey Bellamy lived in Wycombe he had paid two visits to Guernsey, and one to the south of France in 1788 in company with Quaker friends from Philadelphia. In 1800 he again expressed a concern to visit Guernsey, and the "certificate" of approval which it was customary for a MM to provide on these occasions was signed by 24 men and 47 women 'in and on behalf of our MM held at Wycombe', in April 1800.

The numbers attending MM on this occasion may have been exceptional, but they indicate that the Meeting was in a healthy state. They also perhaps reflect the growth of Wycombe as a leading centre in local Quakerism: the Meeting House had recently had major alterations made to it, and acquired new seating;and it was about to house the MM Collection of books, the catalogue of which was published in 1803, showing about 200 titles, and is still available in Friends House Library, London.

After Adey Bellamy's wife died in 1801, he was again 'set at liberty' by the MM to pay a visit to some Meetings in the County of Essex. Unfortunately there are no records of what transpired on these occasions, for it would surely have been interesting to know something of what he saw as the important issues of the day, Quaker or otherwise, about which he may well have spoken. When he died in 1810, after an illness of some two years, he left a legacy for payments 'towards the clothing of apprentices' and to assist 'Friends in limited circumstances to attend their meetings for discipline, when not held at their place of residence'. It was not until 1990 that this fund was finally wound up, with the approval of the Charity Commission.

In about 1804 Wycombe meeting gained a new member in John Wilkinson. He was a son of a clergyman of the Church of England, who died when John was young. His mother had become a Quaker and brought him up as a Friend. He was a young man when he moved to Wycombe, and in 1806 married Esther Wilson of Kendal. They had one daughter, Sarah Wilson, born in 1816, who survived only until 1829. John Wilkinson quickly became very active in the Monthly Meeting, in such ways as signing the testimony to Adey Bellamy in 1810, visiting Friends who "transgressed", and drawing up testimonies of disownment. He "had a gift in the vocal ministry". He was also active in Quarterly Meeting, and paid a religious visit to the Quarterly Meetings of London and Middlesex, Essex and Suffolk; and in Yearly

Meeting, where he became Clerk in 1808, when aged only twenty five, and served until 1814.

In 1830 John Wilkinson was one of a remarkable group of local Friends who are referred to in L. J. Ashford's *History of High Wycombe*.(4) After describing the unhappy state of education in the town in the early 19th Century, Ashford mentions a school-room in old Bassetsbury Manor house where a hundred boys were taught daily by a schoolmaster and a monitor from the London Lancasterian Institute – a body founded by a Quaker, Joseph Lancaster in 1808, which became the British and Foreign Schools Society in 1814. The school had to close in 1828, but was re-opened in 1830 in a hired room in Easton Street as the 'School for Boys on the British System'. Ashford goes on: 'Three Aldermen were included in the reconstituted committee, but of these only Robert Wheeler, the Secretary of the Society, found time to attend the meetings. The other most regular attenders were the Quakers, Thomas Edmonds, William Huntley, John Wilkinson, Richard Lucas and James Thurlow; and a few others....'. The Committee eventually bought and fitted up a building near the church where schools for about 150 boys and 130 girls were opened in 1835.

The PM could not have found a weightier team to represent it on the school committee, and whether or not the Quaker presence was official the team must have had considerable Quaker support. Thomas Edmonds, probably then retired, had been miller of Pann Mill and Rye Mill most of his working life; Richard Lucas, brewer, son-in-law of Thomas Edmonds, who took over Pann Mill for a short period; James Thurlow, owner of Bridge Mill, St. Mary Street; all represent the flourishing business interests of Wycombe Quakers of the day. John Wilkinson was perhaps the epitome of the religious concern of the Society; and William Huntley, brewer and maltster, was Clerk of the PM and a Friend much involved in local Quakerism.

The year 1832 brought, as result of the Reform Act, a general election on a new basis and a wider franchise. 'Quakers in Wycombe ... were well-to-do and locally influential, the Edmonds, the Lucases and the Huntleys, papermakers, brewers and mealmen, and they solidly supported Grey (Whig)'.(5) Thomas Edmonds was active in Whig (shortly to become Liberal) circles, and therefore the object of much virulence from *The Wycombe Sentinel*, a local paper established it seems solely to promote the cause of the other candidate, Benjamin Disraeli. According to the *Sentinel*, 'the objector-general of the Greyites to Mr. Disraeli's voters was Mr. William Grover Edmonds, son of the principal Quaker supporter of Colonel Grey'. 'Have we rid ourselves of the burthen of the old corporation to be the slaves of a junta of Quakers?' thundered the paper. 'It is this favoured sect above all other men, these precisians, with charity ever on their lips, these primitive Christians who have existed only by toleration, and who preach peace while they practice oppression, who have come forward in the present context ...' – a quality of political comment not unknown in the 21st Century. Grey defeated Disraeli, who never stood again for Wycombe; and *The Sentinel* ceased publication immediately.

The account of this period, 1790 into the 1830s, tells of an active Quaker membership who were now looking outward, to members elsewhere, locally, nationally, and even further afield; taking an interest in local needs such as the school and local government; and taking the opportunity offered by the Reform Act also to influence central government. It would have been reasonable to envisage a future of increasing vigour and influence for the Quaker Meeting in High Wycombe. But this conclusion would have been sadly astray.

NOTES TO CHAPTER 6
1. *Dictionary of Quaker Biography*. Friends House Library.
2. L.J. Ashford. *The History of the Borough of High Wycombe*, p.191.
3. John Punshon. *Portrait in Grey. A short history of the Quakers*, p.141.
4. L.J. Ashford. Op cit., p.272 et seq.
5. Ibid, p.265.

CHAPTER 7

The End of the Beginning

QUAKER RECORDS have sometimes been given high praise by County Records Officers, for the care and precision with which they have been kept. But, as we have seen, Monthly Meetings did not make systematic attempts to find out who were their members until the later eighteenth century and actual lists are indeed rare. Thus, for Upperside Monthly Meeting, there is no list earlier than 1820. It is in an exercise book and the entries are alphabetical. They are in clear handwriting, and indicate which Meeting the member attends. Unfortunately, further study reveals that the original document has been added to at later dates than 1820 (probably mostly about 1830 and certainly before 1834), and it is not clear what entries are original and what are not. Moreover, names that should have been on it are not included. Various comments have been added as well (such as 'removed' or 'resigned' or 'deceased') but they do not give a date for the events referred to. However, despite all these idiosyncrasies the list does provide a valuable base on which to build, and an 'edited' version has been prepared.

This list is of all members of whatever age, i.e. including children, and numbers 67. Of these, 47 were female, 20 male. Changes in the period known to have affected each member have been added (Appendix). It is a remarkable table, first because of the glimpse it provides of the constitution of the Meeting at that time; second, because of the sudden drop in the numbers in the ten years to 1830; and finally because further analysis points to reasons for the dramatic decline thereafter. This chapter therefore discusses personalities and families in more detail than any chapters before or after it.

Excluding several deaths in infancy or childhood, as many as 29 members died during this period, 23 of them by 1833. The mortality rate seems to be high, even in the circumstances of the time, and there is no unusual reason to be seen for it. Most deaths were of people of (sometimes remarkably) ripe old age: one was George Orger, who died in 1829, at the age of 80, and was a well-to-do Quaker mealman well before the end of the 18th Century, though his son Thomas seems to have dropped out of the Society. Mary Green, once fond of the 'gay life', as mentioned in Chapter 5, died in 1826 leaving five children who had 'a strict regard for the beliefs and principles of the Society'.[1] She had been elder, overseer and minister from time to time over many years.

Three deaths were early in adult life. There were 17 transfers of membership away from the area, six due to Quaker women marrying Friends elsewhere.

To set against these outgoings of death and removal, though not shown in the table, there were in this period five births in the Green family, though only two of them survived beyond the age of 16;in 1821 two women Friends came to live in Wycombe – Sarah Trendall and Ann Hawgood; and in 1826 the Lucas family arrived, which must have brought great joy to the Meeting. Richard Lucas was the son-in-law of Thomas Edmonds, then 68;Richard had married Elizabeth Edmonds in 1816. His parents were Benjamin and Elizabeth of Westminster, and he was a flour factor at the time. It seems likely that his father-in-law had invited him to share the responsibility of Pann Mill with him, which he did until 1829. Thereafter records show him as a brewer. Richard and Elizabeth had five children at the time of their removal to Wycombe, and others were born later. The family lived at 17 High Street, a building which remains today looking much as it did at that time.

In 1825 William Steevens was reported to the MM to have been married 'by a priest to a person not of our Society' and was visited by John Wilkinson and Sam Edmonds. The MM minute of 7/4/1825 reads that the visitors were 'received with a friendly disposition' and goes on:

> 'But the Friends appointed were not aware of any particular reason why in the present instance the MM should not testify its disunity with such proceeding in the manner it has been used to do in such cases: that the end and design of Friends in a wholesome discipline among us may be answered. The above mentioned Friends are therefore requested to prepare the draft of a testimony against him and bring the same to our next meeting.'

A minute of the next meeting agreed the text of a testimony and went on; 'nevertheless we desire that by manifesting a conduct circumspect and consistent with our religious profession he may become meet to be restored to membership'. Touching though the last sentiment is, it is difficult to imagine how the Meeting expected him to become 'meet to be restored', and as he was the only male Steevens in Quaker membership it seems that the MM had effectively removed a name going back to the very beginning of the Meeting from future membership lists.

Sarah Orger was also disowned, in 1826, but the MM felt very differently about her. She also married a person not in membership, and was reported to be travelling with him and not having any place of residence. She was in due course traced to Norwich, and on being told that she might be disowned expressed herself as being "not concerned at the prospect".

By 1830 the numbers in the Meeting had dropped below 40, but there were still active members in the families of Edmonds, Green, Huntley, Lucas, Steevens, Thurlow and Wilkinson: and this was evident in various ways in the early 1830s. As related in Chapter 6, support was being given to the school in Easton Street. Some Friends were politically active in the general election. John Wilkinson undertook a 'religious visit' to the Quarterly Meetings of London and Middlesex, Essex and Suffolk. William Huntley, in addition to his businesses as a brewer (Frogmore) and maltster (Pauls Row), was clerk of the Meeting and indeed of the Quarterly Meeting for Bucks.

In the years 1836 and 1837 however there were to be various disappointments affecting the Meeting. First, William Huntley's daughter Eliza resigned from the Society. In her letter to the MM she wrote that she had come to the conviction that 'The position in which the Holy Scriptures are placed by the highest authorities in the Society appears to me to be inconsistent with the declarations of the sacred volume itself which I cannot but believe we are bound to accept with heartfelt gratitude as the primary rule of faith and practice, earnestly praying for ability to apprehend the precious truths it contains and to adopt the precepts for our daily guidance'. She ended the letter by stressing the warm attachment she still felt to individual members.

Then in 1837 MM received a resignation from Eliza's brother Richard. He wrote that he had 'long felt much dissatisfaction from attending' worship of the Society of Friends and wished to 'attend somewhere where he might have the benefit of hearing a Gospel ministry'.

In the same year report was made that 'William Huntley has failed in the payment of his just debts', and four members were appointed to visit him, including Thomas Edmonds and James Thurlow. They reported that he had for many years been 'in very embarrassed circumstances; and has gone a most unjustifiable length in business beyond his means. About five years since, when perfectly aware of his insolvency to a very great amount, he entered into a partnership with another person without acquainting him with his real situation'. It was the 'unanimous opinion of the committee that MM cannot do less than testify its disapprobation of such flagrant injustice'. The MM decided with regret to disown him, though expressing the hope that he can 'by sincere repentance and circumspect walking, become meet to be restored to membership'.

Sarah Adams Huntley, William's wife, had died in 1832. The departure in this short period of the whole of the Huntley family, must have been a great shock to the Meeting. Did Sarah's death in some way precipitate what followed? With hindsight is it reasonable to wonder whether the disownment of William was helpful to him or the Meeting? For he was re-instated in 1853, though by that time he was living elsewhere. Was he ever out of sympathy with Friends? Did he, though not in membership, get sympathetic help from the members who knew him so well, and with whom he had been so involved in the Society's work?

The same month that brought Eliza Huntley's resignation also brought one from John Wilkinson. The former must it seems have greatly influenced the latter. He wrote that it was 'now about seven years since I felt a powerful and enduring conviction of the absolute necessity of ... Holy Scripture'. In a long letter he went on:

'The discipline of Friends has served to keep up that normal decency for which they are admired by the world and on account of which they hold themselves in estimation but this is only making clean the outside of the platter, for unless, by Grace of God, Holy Scripture be accepted as the rule of faith and practice there can be no sound internal principle of action, because it is faith in what God has been pleased to reveal through the Apostles and Prophets ... (that is) the foundation upon which all true Christians built. (It) ... is clear that inward and immediate revelation as the Friends understand it is an utter fallacy and to build faith upon what is imagined to be inwardly revealed is nothing better than a delusion'.

His wife Esther wrote at the same time to say that she fully united with her husband's letter. The MM appointed a committee (of which William Huntley was one member!) to prepare a minute of acceptance, and expressed their 'deep sorrow' that the Wilkinsons 'reject the fundamental principle of our Society' but 'affectionately bid them farewell'.

John Wilkinson's huge challenge to the Quaker faith seems quite amazing. Here was a man who had moved in all circles of the Quaker movement for more than thirty years, and as recently as 1832 had travelled widely to promote it. Yet he decides to abandon Quaker faith in a personal relationship with God for a faith in which God is pleased to reveal himself to apostles and prophets but not any more to individual Friends. John Wilkinson's statement in his letter that it was 'about seven years since he had changed his conviction' raises the question whether it was in some way caused by the shock of his young daughter Sarah's death in 1829 at the age of thirteen.

It seems probable that John Wilkinson's resignation was finally prompted by the Yearly Meeting of 1836. Challenged to define the place of the holy scriptures in its faith and practice, it produced a minute which was not strong enough to satisfy the ultra-evangelicals, yet too strong for conservative Friends. A number of Friends resigned, and they included many of Esther Wilkinson's close relatives.

A year later than John Wilkinson's departure the MM was 'informed that Richard Lucas and Elizabeth his wife with some part of his family have for a considerable time ... discontinued attending our religious meetings, and have attended and continue to attend another place of worship'. Two Friends were appointed to visit them and were 'kindly received' but there was no change in the situation, so a further visit was made. Their report said that 'it was evident that they were dissatisfied with the mode of worship observed by Friends' though 'much was expressed by Richard Lucas which we conceived to be in great measure foreign to the subject'. There was no indication that he and his wife shared the evangelical conviction now embraced by John Wilkinson. With regret Richard and Elizabeth Lucas were disowned, with an expression of Friends' 'love for them and an earnest desire for their present and eternal well-being'.

Specific reference to the position of the numerous Lucas children, then of ages between 10 and 20 years, was not made. Some of them may have continued to attend meetings occasionally, but they would need to have had strong convictions to do so: their grandmother Elizabeth Edmonds had died in 1836, and many of the aunts and uncles from the Edmonds family had left home or died, so family ties to the Meeting would probably not have kept them. By 1852 all of the Lucases had resigned or been disowned.

The events so far described, of the late 1830s in Wycombe Meeting, must have been disheartening: but there was encouragement in the arrival in 1837 of John Huntley, whose membership had been in Witney MM. He was born in Burford, Oxfordshire, in 1784, and initially became a biscuit baker, though on his removal to Wycombe was an accountant. He was unmarried, and there is no indication that he was related to the Huntleys who, until recently, had been members of Wycombe Meeting. He quickly became active in local Quaker circles, and was appointed clerk of the PM in 1838. He was to have an important part to play for over 30 years, but was not to know that the Meeting was about to go into serious decline. The stories, in the years following 1840, of those families who have already been described as the pillars of the Meeting, illustrate vividly why this was so.

There were two branches of the Edmonds family, both with long Quaker membership. Thomas Edmonds was about 80 when John Huntley arrived. His wife Elizabeth had died only recently, in 1836. Their only son, William Grover, unmarried, died in 1837. Four daughters had married and left home before that. For fifteen years Thomas and one daughter, Rebecca, were the only members of the family left in the Meeting. Thomas died in 1851 at his home in Easton Street, at the age of 93. The Census of 1851 showed his household to consist of housekeeper, cook, and housemaid. Rebecca promptly married in 1852 and moved away.

The other branch was headed by Samuel and his wife Grizzell, a daughter of Mary Green mentioned above. Their two daughters had long since married and left home. Samuel died in 1848.

The Green family was similarly depleted. In 1840 only Ann and William remained of the children of Mary. Ann was single, living alone, in Crendon Lane. She died in 1844. William's wife Susanna had died in 1838, leaving two young children: but William himself died in 1842, and the two children before long were sent to live in the midlands. So no Greens remained thereafter.

The Steevens family, bereft of the membership of William who had been disowned in 1825, consisted of Elizabeth, then of considerable age; and her daughters Mary, 56, and Anna, 42. Elizabeth died in 1841. In 1848 Anna married John Huntley, which must have startled the Meeting. So Mary remained, living with the Huntleys in the High Street.

Finally the Thurlow family, who might have been expected to give solid support for many years. As seen on the list, James and Lydia had two children, James jnr. and Sarah. But Lydia died in 1845, and her husband moved away in 1849. James jnr., clearly unhappily, resigned in 1854 because he wanted to marry someone not in membership: he remained in Wycombe, took an active part in local government, and in due course became an alderman. No further record of Sarah has been found.

In 1851 there was a unique Census of Religious Worship throughout the country. For the Society of Friends in High Wycombe the return, made by John Huntley, showed that on 30th March there were eleven people present at the morning Meeting for Worship and four in the afternoon. On that date, *members* amounted to no more than eight, so the others were either visitors from elsewhere, or local non-members who today might be described as 'attenders'. No records are available to show the numbers, let alone the names, at any one time, of those who might be as regular at Meeting as members, but who – sadly for the Meeting – never felt able to join. They might give some practical or financial help, but could not, for example, be clerk, treasurer, elder, overseer or minister, or represent the Meeting at Monthly or other business meetings of the Society. So their names would not appear in any official records of appointments.

Unfortunately the first chance of identifying attenders of those days is when they were dead. Some of them are probably among non-members who were buried in the Quaker burial ground in Wycombe. Indeed it is probable that non-members who made this their place of burial were predominantly people who had been attending Meeting. In the years 1820-1870 they numbered 21, though only five of them were recorded after 1850.

Clearly the Meeting was now very small. In considering the reasons for its catastrophic decline mention might be made of the enormous preponderance of girls over boys in the growing families of the 1820s and 1830s. That the girls became attractive women is evident from the vast numbers who married and moved away;but there were no young men in Wycombe Meeting at the time, William Steevens and James Thurlow jnr. having been forced from membership by the rule against 'marrying out'.

Wycombe may have been unlucky at this time in the numbers who moved away, though its losses will have been gains in other Meetings. The numbers of disownments however, so often blamed for the decline of the society as a whole, cannot be regarded as of overwhelming importance. The predominant facts are that no members moved in, and no one was taken into membership. The decline can only be explained by a fall of sympathy at that time for what the Meeting stood for.

Not that Wycombe was exceptional in its decline. In Aylesbury the Meeting House had been closed in 1837. In Amersham Meetings for Worship were discontinued in 1850, and in Chesham in 1857. Only Berkhamsted retained some strength. Monthly Meeting itself suffered, attendance as early as 1845 having dropped to twelve. In 1857 the MM agreed to join with Leighton MM (Bedfordshire) to form a new Upperside and Leighton MM. National figures make it clear that membership of the Society had been declining for a considerable time, and reached its lowest in 1860.

By 1864 the only Friends remaining in Wycombe were Grizzell Edmonds, John Huntley and his wife Anna. John had transferred his solid support to the new MM, and remained a frequent attender at Quarterly Meeting: but he was finding the travel increasingly difficult, and the Meeting decided that it would be much easier to look south and west rather than north and east – the railway from Wycombe to Maidenhead had been opened in 1847 and such thinking had become increasingly common in the town. In 1866 the PM left Upperside and Leighton and joined Reading and Warborough MM. In 1867 afternoon meetings were discontinued, 'considering the smallness of our numbers and infirmities attendant on advanced years', and in 1868 it was sometimes impossible for anyone to get even to the morning meeting.

The year 1869 brought the death of Grizzell Edmonds: she was 95. The *Free Press*, not in those days accustomed to reporting funerals, made an exception. A large number of friends and relatives, it related, formed a procession from the house in the High Street to the grave, where two 'brief and suitable' addresses were delivered. The gathering then adjourned to the Meeting House, where 'Mr. Dell again spoke, Mr. Huntley engaged in prayer', and 'Mr. J. Bourne of Reading gave an address'. There is no doubt that Grizzell Edmonds deserved exceptional attention: she had clearly been an unwavering strength to family, Society and Meeting over probably seventy years.

The Huntleys however were not defeated. The Meeting continued and on 11th September 1870 they appointed themselves representatives to attend Monthly Meeting at Reading, the first and only time representatives had been sent since 1865. But Anna died before the end of the year, Wycombe Meeting officially closed, and John Huntley moved to live with one of his relatives, Joseph Huntley, at Kendrick Road, Reading. Anna was buried in Wycombe Burial

Ground, and John spent some of his last days making a plan of the graves there, including that of his wife. He died shortly after, on 18th December 1871. The *Free Press* wrote a short tribute to his life in Wycombe in its issue of 22nd December.

So ends a sad story, perhaps leaving the reader with enormous sympathy for the last few Friends and particularly for John Huntley, who came unexpectedly when the Meeting was suffering from defections, and saw it move inexorably downwards over 30 years to the position where it had to close. For most, if not all, of those years he was its Clerk. It was the end of the first 200 years of Quakerism, but from it new conceptions were to grow, and it was far from being the end of Quakerism in High Wycombe.

NOTE TO CHAPTER 7
1. *Dictionary of Quaker Biography*, Friends House Library, on Joseph Green.

Appendix

Membership of High Wycombe Meeting 1820 and changes 1820-1840

SURNAME	FIRST NAME	BIRTH	CHANGES 1820-1840
BEALE	WILLIAM		Removed 1826
BEVAN	PRISCILLA	c.1757	Died 1824
DREWETT	BERYL		Resigned 1836
EDMONDS	THOMAS	c.1758	
EDMONDS	ELIZABETH	1771	Died 1836. Wife of Thomas
EDMONDS	RACHEL		Died before 1834. Daughter of Thomas
EDMONDS	PRISCILLA		Removed (marriage) 1827. Daughter of Thomas
EDMONDS	SARAH		Removed (marriage) 1835. Daughter of Thomas
EDMONDS	WILLIAM GROVER	1805	Died 1837. Son of Thomas
EDMONDS	JANE		Removed (marriage) 1835. Daughter of Thomas
EDMONDS	REBECCA		Daughter of Thomas
EDMONDS	SAMUEL		
EDMONDS	GRIZZELL		Wife of Samuel
EDMONDS	GRIZZELL MARY		Removed (marriage) 1827. Daughter of Samuel
EDMONDS	ANNA		Removed (marriage) 1832. Daughter of Samuel
ENDALL	ELIZABETH	1744	Died 1827
ENDALL	SAMUEL		Died 1827

SURNAME	FIRST NAME	BIRTH	CHANGES 1820-1840
FAGE	MEHETABEL	1754	Died 1821
GREEN	MARY	c.1747	Died 1826. Widow of Joseph
GREEN	ANN	1776	Daughter of Joseph & Mary
GREEN	WILLIAM	1783	Son of Joseph & Mary
GREEN	SUSANNA	1786	Died 1838. Wife of William
GREEN	MARY	1820	Died 1839. Daughter of William & Susanna
HOLLAND	ROBERT		Died before 1834
HUNT	MARY		Removed 1825
HUNT	JOHN		Removed before 1834
HUNT	ELIZABETH	1793	Died 1829
HUNT	WILLIAM		Removed before 1834
HUNTLEY	SARAH ADAMS	1808	Died 1834
HUNTLEY	WILLIAM		Disowned (business conduct) 1837
HUNTLEY	ELIZABETH		Resigned 1836. Daughter of William
HUNTLEY	RICHARD		Resigned 1837. Son of William
LAMLEY	JOHN	1784	Died 1822
LAMLEY	SARAH		Removed 1822. Brother of John
LAMLEY	SAMUEL		Removed before 1834
LINE	ANN	1764	Died 1835
ORGER	GEORGE	c.1749	Died 1829
ORGER	SARAH	1753	Died 1823. Wife of George
ORGER	SARAH		Disowned (marrying out) 1826. Daughter of George
PATTISSON	SARAH	1740	Died 1823
PHILPS	HANNAH		Removed 1821
PHILPS	SUSANNA		Removed 1821
POLLEY	MARY ANN	1771	Died 1831
ROBINSON	SARAH		Removed before 1834
STEEVENS	MARY		Died before 1834
STEEVENS	REBEKAH		Died before 1834
STEEVENS	ANN		Died before 1834
STEEVENS	ELIZABETH		Died 1829
STEEVENS	ELIZABETH		Widow of Joseph
STEEVENS	MARY Jnr.	<1792	Daughter of Elizabeth
STEEVENS	WILLIAM		Disowned (marrying out) 1825. Son of Elizabeth
STEEVENS	SARAH		Removed (marriage) 1832. Daughter of Elizabeth
STEEVENS	ANNA	>1792	Daughter of Elizabeth
THURLOW	JAMES		
THURLOW	LYDIA		Wife of James
THURLOW	JAMES Jnr.		
THURLOW	SARAH		
TRENDALL	LUCY	1764	Died 1827
WALDUCK	SARAH	1749	Died 1829. Widow (of John?)
WALDUCK	JOHN	1744	Died 1820
WELLS	HENRY		Removed before 1834
WHEELER	LUCY	1770	Removed 1823
WILKINSON	MARTHA	1741	Died 1821
WILKINSON	JOHN		Resigned 1836
WILKINSON	ESTHER		Resigned 1836. Wife of John
WILKINSON	SARAH	1816	Died 1829. Daughter of John
YOUNG	ELEANOR	1749	Died 1829. Widow of John

CHAPTER 8

New Roots

THE STORY OF Quakerism in High Wycombe begins again with another death of another Steevens. Elizabeth Steevens was born in 1826. She was the first child born to William, who had been disowned for marrying a non-member in 1825. She died in 1913, then living in Crendon Lane. There is no record of her parents having continued to attend the Meeting after her father's disownment, and Elizabeth herself never joined the Society, but she must have had lifelong warm recollections of it, for she had expressed a wish that her funeral service might be conducted in the Friends Meeting House, and that she be buried in the Friends burial ground.

The Meeting House and cottage had been leased out in 1879 for a period of 42 years, and the former was being used in 1913 as a schoolroom by Christ Church, on the opposite side of the lane. Approval had therefore to be obtained from the Vicar and Churchwardens and this was readily given. The service was in accordance with Wesleyan Methodist practice, and conducted by two ministers of that church, to which Elizabeth presumably belonged.

The *Free Press* wrote a lengthy report of the funeral. Its reference to the interment is of particular interest:

'The interment took place in the quaint and secluded burial ground, sacred to the memory of many generations of local Friends, which is situated in Railway-place. The enclosure is about 90 feet square, and is surrounded by a high brick wall, with an entrance from Station-road. It has been used for the interment of Quakers from about the year 1682, and no fewer than five generations of the Steevens' family have been buried there.'

Plans of the ground were closely examined by Cally Trench in 1998 when the archives were displayed in the Meeting House. She estimated that at the time the Meeting closed in 1870 there had been about 150 interments. After that date at least three people were buried there before Elizabeth Steevens. (None of them were members, but all had family already buried there).

There is no detail of the location of burials before 1748, though the first section of the ground was leased in 1663, and Quarterly Meeting records of burials ("mostly in Wycombe") start in 1664. An explanation of this may lie in the fact that there was Advice from Yearly Meeting in 1766, referring back to that of 1717, to the effect that 'monuments already in being over dead bodies of Friends should be removed ... and that none be anywhere made or set up, near or over the dead bodies of Friends and others, in Friends' burying places for time to come'. It is therefore possible that early monuments were removed sometime after 1717, but before a plan of burials began to be kept in 1748. In 1850, Yearly Meeting agreed that headstones could be put up, provided that the inscription contained only a name and dates. There were some headstones remaining in the burial ground at the time it was given to the Council.

The burial of Elizabeth Steevens was a significant event in the history of Wycombe Quakers because it turned out to be the last to take place in the burial ground, and because she herself was the last link with the membership of the first Meeting. It may also have some significance because of the warmth and prominence of the news item which it prompted in the *Free Press*. This would certainly have encouraged those who placed the notice in the paper a year later which read: 'A Meeting for worship after the manner of Friends will be held every Sunday at 6.30 p.m. at the Old Meeting House, Crendon Lane, until further notice. Friends and all interested will be welcome'.

Life in the Wycombe of 1913 was of course different from that of 1870. Whereas in 1861 John Huntley and his wife and sister-in-law lived in the High Street, next door to Grizzell Edmonds, and a few doors away from the large and prosperous, though no longer Quaker, Lucas household, by 1900 these and many other domestic properties in the street had become business premises. By 1913 there were very few private households listed, and change of this kind had also taken place in Crendon Lane, Elizabeth Steevens' house being the last to be recorded as such. Crendon Lane was still very narrow, but the importance of the fact that it led to the railway station was increased in 1906 by the opening of the railway line to Marylebone. (Until then rail access to London had been via Maidenhead.)

During the last years of the century, the town centre was probably getting more unpleasant to live in. 'Sewers' at that time comprised open drains and ditches, and Ashford describes the situation as found by the Medical Officer of Health whose appointment had been forced upon the borough by legislation of 1871:

> 'The borough's Medical Officer reported that the drainage and water supply of the whole town were bad. The wells in nearly every part were polluted. Such sewers as existed were quite inadequate because they had practically no fall. The health of the town was good, except for some outbreaks of smallpox. But if an epidemic should come, "there is plenty of food for it to feed upon".'

The then borough boundaries limited the practicability of a sewage scheme. The answer was to extend the boundaries, doubling the population to 10,000 people, and it was not therefore until 1901 that a satisfactory sewerage scheme had been put in place. The town centre would have been pleasanter as result, though in 1907 the first motor bus came into service, and residents began to complain of the noise, vibration and fumes coming from this source!

In the country as a whole there had been significant social changes affecting family and community life. The Education Act of 1871 brought universal primary education. All adult men had the parliamentary vote though women had yet to receive it, and militant suffragettes appeared on the scene. Middle class girls no longer stayed at home and awaited marriage, and many of them worked in offices, comprising, for example, 40% of all employees in typewriting and telephone services by 1900. (G.K.Chesterton was later to refer to the millions of young women who ' ... declared that they would not be dictated to, and then went out and became stenographers').

There was, according to G.M. Trevelyan, 'free debate of social customs and religious beliefs ... taking the place of the settled creeds of the early Victorian era'.[1] Church attendance had steadily declined, rather more than did attendance at chapel: an estimate for 1902-3 is that in small towns regular "churchgoers" comprised about 25% of the population.

There had also been considerable change in the nature of Quakerism itself. No longer was there the witness, maintained by some Friends to the bitter end, against the payment of church rates and tithes. The Tithe Redemption Act of 1836 did not affect the essential character of tithes, but converted them into a fixed charge on land. Friends were divided on whether or not this should be paid, and it was not until 1873 that Yearly Meeting removed its official opposition. The liability to pay church rates was removed by law in 1878.

More importantly, in 1859 the Yearly Meeting had permitted marriages to non-members, thus staunching one cause of serious loss of members, though not in time to affect the decline of the then Meeting in Wycombe. Even more important again, was the gradual acceptance by Friends of liberal theology and biblical criticism, the rejection in fact of the evangelicalism which had led to the resignation of John Wilkinson and others in 1836. This acceptance of a new approach to Quaker faith culminated in 1895, when a thousand Friends gathered in Manchester to discuss its implications for the movement. Yearly Meeting was reconstituted in 1896 to include women Friends, though women had had their own YM since 1784, and Upperside MM was a joint meeting of men and women in the 1850s.

Credit must be given at this point to the part played in the latter part of the 19th Century by the evangelicals in the Society, in promoting Quaker involvement in humanistic and social causes, such as the liberation of slaves and the formation of Adult Schools. Humanitarian movements were taken warmly into Quaker life and remain so today. At this time Quakers frequently entered parliament. In 1880 ten were elected, and at subsequent elections up to 1910 the numbers were all in double figures.

In 1920 a book was published which came to be greatly respected for many years thereafter. It was *The Faith of a Quaker* by John W. Graham. In his preface the author writes that the book was written during the few years preceding the first World War, and was in the hands of the printers when the war stopped publication. It is thus a book which exactly spans the period of formation of the new Meeting in High Wycombe. At the end the author wrote:

> 'In this generation a revolution has come over the face of our own and other churches. Once more the gospel of the Inward Life and Light is restored. If we obey it and live in it with sufficient power and concentrated service, the prophetic ministry must surely break forth as its expression ... We are now in the morning of another day, and the time for the expression of our faith is this time'.[2]

The new Meeting it seems was founded in this sort of spirit, and it led quickly to a weekend gathering on 'Quakerism and Modern Life', reported in the *Free Press* of May 1st 1914 as follows:

> 'A revival of Quakerism is undoubtedly taking place in the South Bucks district, in which the memory of revered names and honoured stalwarts in the cause is personally cherished. The establishment of a Guest House at Jordans within the last few years has contributed largely to the spirit of revivalism, which has enlisted the sympathy and support of neighbouring counties and of visit-

ing members of the Society of Friends from all parts, as well as from America. At High Wycombe, which was in times gone by a centre of the Friends' activity, there is a distinct resuscitation of the cause, and religious services are held from time to time in the Old Meeting House, Crendon-street (by kind permission of Canon J. Rushby Smith there). On Saturday afternoon, at half past four, a meeting took place when an address was given on 'Quakerism and Modern Life' by Mrs. Barbara McKenzie ... Mr. Edward Brown of Luton presided.' (A long report followed).

Jordans Meeting House had re-opened in 1911 after about a century of closure, but it was not until the 1920s that Meetings re-appeared in Amersham and Aylesbury, and it was later still that Chesham followed. Nevertheless membership of the Society as a whole was slowly picking up. In Wycombe the notice in the *Free Press* about the revival of Meetings for Worship at the Meeting House was the result of a 'pilot' meeting held on 4th January 1914. *The Friend* of 9th January 1914 reported:

'A London Friend has recently moved to Wycombe and made arrangements for a meeting for worship to be held in the old haunt of Friends. The first meeting (announced in the paper and by a few posters) was held last Sunday evening, a few Friends from Jordans and elsewhere being present, besides some fifty local people. So large an attendance was quite a surprise, and the meeting served to show how the memory of Friends lingers on in south or "upperside" Buckinghamshire. It is intended to continue to hold meetings, either in the morning or evening.'

An attendance sheet was signed by sixteen of those who were present (Appendix I). Five of them are Friends identifiably from the Monthly Meeting, there to give encouragement. The only 'London Friend recently removed to High Wycombe' was Katherine Parker, so it seems likely that she was the one who had taken the initiative.

During 1914 the Monthly Meeting (Luton and Leighton at that time) showed great interest in the matter, and also made a grant of £8 per annum available: the Quarterly Meeting noted that the meeting had 'drawn into fellowship a number of thoughtful people not previously connected with the Society of Friends', and gave it official status as an 'Allowed Meeting' under the auspices of Jordans Preparative Meeting. (This meant that it had responsibility only for the Meeting for Worship and not necessarily for other aspects of local Quaker work, which would be a responsibility of the business meeting at Jordans).

The Quarterly Meeting list of High Wycombe members for 1915 is reproduced in Appendix II. It shows that by then there were 10 members on it, and 28 'attenders' (people who came to Meeting for Worship but had not joined the Society). However, the names of Friends from Aylesbury, Buckingham and Haddenham would be on the list only because of there being no Meeting nearer to them: it is unlikely that they could play an active part. That left six local members who could be asked to accept responsibilities. Though little is known about the others listed, mainly new to Friends, their addresses indicate that they were mostly 'middling people'. Most too lived within walking distance of the Meeting House, in contrast to the situation nowadays, though Flackwell Heath and The Marsh would make attendance at Meeting more difficult. One of them, Sarah Steevens, could hardly be described as 'new to Friends': she was a niece of Elizabeth Steevens, with whose name this chapter opened, and she lived at 30 Crendon Lane, only a few doors away from where her aunt lived, and from the Meeting House itself. She had clearly retained the family interest in the Society, and continued to do so, for thirty five years later (in 1950) she was to display, for the benefit of members, 'a collection of objects such as clothing, manuscripts etc. illustrative of the life of Friends in days gone by'.

From quite early on the new Meeting showed that it had wide interests when it decided to arrange 'Fellowship Meetings', if possible in the evening of every first Sunday in the month, open to all and publicised in the *Free Press*. At each meeting there would be a speaker and opportunities for discussion on the subject of the address. Six meetings had been arranged up to the end of 1915, and after that nine per year was the norm (Appendix III). It is interesting that Neave Brayshaw, who attended the first meeting in 1914, spoke at several Fellowship Meetings. He was already becoming well known as a writer on the Quaker faith, and his close links with Wycombe meeting for many years would be a great strength to it.

The Meeting's concern with matters of war and peace is clear from the subjects of Fellowship Meetings chosen through the war years – e.g. 'Heroism and Peace' 1915; 'The world in the making' and 'The coming of the Kingdom' 1917; 'The coming of Peace', 'Friends work among war victims in Holland', 'Preparing the world for the future', and 'Friends work in France' 1918; and – after the war was over – 'Afterwards' and 'Visions of the New World'. Numbers attending these Fellowship Meetings would be considered impressive by today's standards – averaging over 25 and occasionally reaching nearly 40. In today's computer world one wonders, for comparison, how many visits to the website of a small Quaker meeting there would be.

To back up these meetings a small lending library was formed in 1917, and in 1918 it was agreed that Katherine Parker should prepare a pamphlet, on Wycombe Meeting House and Quaker principles, for local distribution – though no evidence that this was achieved has survived.

The war itself must have been much on the minds of members of the Meeting. From the beginning Wycombe was a billeting area, and 2000 military personnel were quartered there. In 1916 the Military Service Act came into force, opposed at national level with vigour by the Friends Service Committee, and tribunals were set up in each locality with responsibility for considering the cases of those who asked for deferment on grounds of hardship or exemption on grounds of conscience. There is no evidence that any of the latter were members of the Meeting.

Bedfordshire General Meeting reported to the central Wartime Statistics Committee that three members of one family from Penn had at first all been rejected for military service during the war on grounds of poor health, but two had later been accepted and sent to France in the army in 1917. They were Arnold Maurice Day and Cecil Gordon Day, both members, and Henry Day, an attender. The last two mentioned were those who were finally called up. George North, closely involved in the new meeting from the beginning, was rejected by the National Service Medical Board as totally unfit for military service.

Though Wycombe Friends were not personally involved in the activities of the tribunals, other members of the Monthly Meeting certainly were, and in March 1916 the MM minuted as follows:

'It appears that Members of our Society are generally receiving much more lenient treatment at the tribunals than other conscientious objectors, and we must therefore do our best to give these our support by prayer and encouragement or in any way possible, and it is suggested that our merely being present in a sympathetic spirit at the tribunals may be of great help to them, even though no one may speak thereat without special leave.

We must also be careful that we do not encourage the idea that our young Friends care only about saving themselves from conscription, and do not mind about anything further'.

A little later an unexpected participant in a wider debate about the treatment of conscientious objectors by the tribunals was Lord

Parmoor. As Charles Alfred Cripps, (whose address was Parmoor, Frieth, near High Wycombe) before he was ennobled, he was Conservative MP for Wycombe from 1910 to 1914. He wrote to *The Times* in 1917, quoting the Prime Minister at the debate on the Military Service Act, when he had said "All men whose objections to active military service are founded on honest convictions ought to be able, and will be able, to avail themselves of the exemptions which Parliament has provided". The Minister in charge of the Bill at that moment had said: 'I do not want, and nobody in the Government wants, the horror of men who for conscience sake are unwilling to serve being thrown into gaol for a long time'. 'Yet', wrote Lord Parmoor, 'this horror is a matter of everyday occurrence'.

The *Free Press* quoted Lord Parmoor's letter in full in its columns, side by side with 'A Reply' from the Chairman of the Surrey Appeal Tribunal. Though local papers were reported to have invited the mauling or mobbing of 'C.Os.'[3] it has to be said that the Free Press throughout maintained an admirable balance in its reporting.

Parmoor married a Quaker, Marian Ellis, in 1919 and was to be a prominent member of the Labour governments of 1924 and 1929-31, being made specially responsible for League of Nations affairs in 1924.

During its first five years the Meeting grew steadily, and by 1920 it recorded 21 members and 23 attenders. Katherine Parker, the originating member and first 'correspondent' (i.e. responsible for communications on behalf of the group), had good support from Jane North, Arthur Whitlow – though he left Wycombe in 1915 – and probably Simeon and Jane Hunt. Davina Watkins, who had been associated with the Society since childhood, joined in 1915. A little later came Walter Houghton, George Small (a chairmaker, who said he had been 'interested' for 12 years) and – in 1920 – George North (husband of Jane). When the latter joined reference was made to 'his helpful vocal service in High Wycombe Meeting, raising the standard of its sincerity and simplicity'.

Early in 1921 the Meeting suggested to the MM that it could be established as a Preparative Meeting, but the matter was deferred in view of the fact that the lease of the Meeting House to Christ Church was about to run out. However in September both Monthly and Quarterly Meetings had agreed that this should not be an obstacle. The MM firmly refused a request from the churchwardens for an extension of the lease, and Wycombe became a Preparative Meeting with full responsibilities.

NOTES TO CHAPTER 8
1. G.M. Trevelyan. *English Social History*, p.551.
2. John W. Graham. *The Faith of a Quaker*, p.415.
3. G.D.H. Cole and Raymond Postgate. *The Common People*, p.525.

Appendix I – Attendance sheet of 'pilot' meeting of 1914.

HIGH WYCOMBE
(ALLOWED MEETING)
(In Jordans P.M)
Crendon Lane

10 Members. 28 Attenders.

Katherine Parker (Mrs.), (Correspondent)
Temple Orchard, High Wycombe.

Meeting for Worship: 1st day, at 6.30 p.m.

Railway Station: High Wycombe (G.C. G.W.R. Joint) ¼ mile

Market: 6th-day

- (*) Booth (Mrs.), Hughenden Valley
- (-) Dairy (Mrs.), Kate, Hughenden Valley
- (*) Daniel (Miss), Olive, 57, Priory Avenue
- (*) Derwent (Miss), M. A., Cowgra Road
- Dunn (Miss), Ivy, Bermalipe, King's Road, [Aylesbury
- (-) Hausen, Daniel, 135, Hughenden Road
- (*) Holland (Mr.), 152, Desborough Road
- (*) Hogarths (Miss), Gabriel, 22, Benjamin [Road
- (*) Houghton, Walter,
- Hunt, Simeon, Woodview, Penn Road, [Hazlemere
- Hunt (Mrs.)
- (*) Kendall, P. H., White Hart Street
- (*) Kendall (Miss), Gabrielle, White Hart Street
- (*) North, George, Oakridge Lodge, West [Wycombe Road
- North, Jane
- (-) Edward Samuel Lithgow
- (-) Hector
- (-) Peter
- Parish (Mrs.), Katherine, Temple Orchard, [Amersham Hill
- (*) Parker, Charles A.
- (-) Robert
- Perry (Mrs.), Alice, Wharf Side Cottages, [Stratford Road, Buckingham
- Rose, Walter, Aston Road, Haddenham, [Bucks.
- Rose, Mary Louisa
- Elsie Mary
- Ivor Frederick
- Marjorie Doris
- (*) Salter, W. E., Golf View, Blackwell Heath, [Loudwater
- (-) Salter (Mrs.)
- (*) Salter (Miss), Gladys
- (*) Stevens (Miss), Sarah, 30, Crendon Lane
- (*) Thorpe (Mr.), 2, Vandyck Villas, [Desborough Park Road
- (*) Thorpe (Mrs.)
- (*) Walter (Miss), Kingswood, The Marsh
- (*) Wurms (Miss), Daisy, Edgemont, [Rectory Avenue
- (*) Watts, George, 25, Railway Place
- (-) Watts (Mrs.)
- (*) Watts, Harry, Eaton, Roberts Road
- (*) Watts (Mrs.)
- (*) Whitton, Arthur, Home

Appendix II – High Wycombe Allowed Meeting 1915.

Appendix III

Fellowship Meetings

Date	Subject	Speaker	Att.
1914			
1/11	Are we contented?	Roland Warren	25
6/12	The message of Llandudno	Malcolm Sparkes	36
1915			
7/2	Heroism and Peace	St. John Catchpool	27
3/10		Stephen Gloyne	
7/11		Janet Payne	25
5/12	What Nurse Cavell saw	Miss Helen Ward	38
1916			
2/1		Roderic Clarke	24
5/3		Neave Brayshaw	38
2/4		Henry Harris	20
7/5		Neave Brayshaw	38
4/6	The sermon on the mount	Frederic Taylor	30
9/7	Friends work in France	Egbert Morland	28
1/10		Rowntree Gillett	38
5/11	Friends Foreign Mission	D.H. Hodgkin	26
3/12	The struggle for religious freedom in Bucks. 17th Century	Anna Littleboy	28
1917			
7/1	The Fellowship of the Church, its nature & object	Neave Brayshaw	33
4/2	The world in the making	Alfred Lynn	20
4/3	A Quaker view of Socialism	Rosa Hobhouse	
1/4	St. Francis of Assisi	Annie Wright	30
6/5	Inspiration and industry	Rosa Hobhouse	
3/6		J. Perry Fletcher	22
7/10	The message	Albert Cotterell	22
4/11	The coming of the Kingdom	Marion Ellis	38
2/12	The churches and Social Order	C.R. Simpson	
1918			
6/1	The coming of Peace	Henrietta Thomas	24
3/2	Friends work among war victims in Holland	Reginald Price	34
3/3	Preparing the World for the Future	Wm. Loftus Hare	20
7/4	Spiritual reformers	W.A. Caffell	20
5/5	Friends work in France	Miss Daniels	
2/6	Yearly Meeting	Katherine Parker	
3/11	Y.W.C.A. work	Miss Standish	
1/12	Afterwards	Barrington Whitlow	
1919			
5/1	Visions of the New World	Percy Stranger	14
2/2	Lessons from the life of Tolstoy	Esther M. Kitching	
2/3	The Missionary Work of the Society		
6/4	The rebirth of man through war	Charles Knight	
1/6	The message of Yearly Meeting	Mrs. Watkins	20
5/10	Whitley Councils	Malcolm Sparkes	

65

CHAPTER 9

Househunting

IN KATHERINE PARKER and Jane North the new Meeting chose two redoubtable women to lead it as Clerk and Assistant Clerk. Both had already given it much help and were well placed to give more. The families were certainly well-to-do, living within a proverbial stones' throw of each other on Amersham Hill, and their husbands gave them excellent support. The first business meeting was held at the home of Jane North in September 1921. With fourteen people present they must all have felt very encouraged. The official List of Members is shown in the Appendix.

Probably none of them could have foreseen how their deliberations were to be dominated by responsibility for property, or for how long. The Town Council informed them in December that it would not take over the graveyard, because too much would have to be spent on it, and its care was to prove an irksome liability on the Meeting: and in March 1922 came another shock when Steevens, builders, gave them an estimate of £675 for the cost of dilapidations at the Meeting House at the end of the lease to Christ Church.

The Church repudiated the claim for dilapidations, and at the Monthly Meeting's request the Meeting House was locked up for the time being, but the MM was pressed to take urgent action 'forthwith'. Eventually £160 was accepted from the Church, and the property was sold to the Council for £2,250 'with a clause to the effect that the sale is for street widening only'.

'First Aid' must have been given to the premises, and a temporary arrangement made with the Council, for meetings continued to be held at the Meeting House. There were '29 oak forms' there (still used by some today!) which had been bought well before the sale of the property, so seating was available. In March 1923 an application from Christ Church Sunday School for the use of one room was approved; and thought was even being given to a 'small reconstruction scheme'

66

though this never materialised. 'As a subject of historic interest', MM recorded the demolition of the property in March 1930.

Despite the difficulties with premises public meetings were also held. In April 1925 PM at Crendon Lane recorded 'that during the past winter the Fellowship Meetings were held on First day evenings. Subjects: The Home; The School; Leisure; The Church; The World of Industry; Property; Work; Distribution; The World of Nations; The Heart of the Matter. Five Meetings of a Study Circle met on weekday evenings to consider and discuss the 'Copec' publication *Property and Industry*. The new PM was certainly as outward looking as the Allowed Meeting which it succeeded.

During this time negotiations for another property were going on, and the last business meeting of 1924 recorded that the lease of the Mission Hall, Corporation Street, had been transferred to the Society, and agreement made to purchase the furniture there. The deeds refer to 'all that building ... intended to be used as a Hall for religious purposes (which) was demised unto the lessees from 25 December 1908 for 21 years'. The vendors agreed to sell the residue of the lease (i.e. until the end of 1929) for the price of £93.19.0.

The first PM at the Meeting House at Corporation Street was dated 3rd January 1925, and members had much to do making it suitable for its new purpose. On 10th January 1926 thanks were recorded, to Sam North (an architect, eldest son of George) 'for lettering the large sign which hangs outside the building, and the notice boards'; to George North 'for having the original Elder's Bench so effectively and successfully renovated'; and to George Small (who was a chairmaker) 'for preparing the foot rests and for other work'.

No sooner were the new premises in use than the Meeting arranged more public meetings bringing into prominence the view that Christianity in general, and Quakerism in particular, had a relevance to issues of the day. In 1925 there were six special addresses on their relevance to rural problems; in 1926 there were four lectures on Quakerism by Katherine Parker; and in 1927 four on more specific aspects -

1) Fred Tritton on International Service
2) Charles Stanfield on Education and Friends Schools
3) Katherine Innes on Friends Peace Committee
4) George Small on Early Friends.

A new Monthly Meeting ('Jordans') was created in 1925, covering approximately the original area of Upperside MM of the early days of the Society, and it decided to hold its first meeting at Corporation Street on 12th January 1926. Thereafter meetings were to be held alternatively in Wycombe, Jordans or Amersham. Wycombe was now regarded as giving solid support to the MM, and the official records ('Tabular Statements') show its membership to have been steady at 16 or 17 during the years 1926-1929, additionally with about 11 attenders.

By 1929 the PM was becoming anxious again about premises. The lease at Corporation Street would expire at the end of the year, and the room there was not proving very satisfactory. Minutes in 1927 and 1928 about buying a Valor oil stove, about repairs to the 'furnace', and about gratitude for 'gifts of firewood from George North' show that heating was not perfect; and a report to MM referred to the room being 'unattractive'. This was thought to have been a cause of the ebbing attendances at evening meetings, which were eventually discontinued. Monthly Meeting decided not to renew the lease, and appointed a committee to work with local Friends to obtain 'suitable temporary accommodation' and to look for something permanent for the future.

At the end of the year accommodation was found in 'rooms' at 'The Limes' in Easton Street, for a rent of £1 per week. This was a rather sombre looking house on the North side, with 'CONSERVATIVE PARTY' proclaimed in an upper window. Some of the furniture from Corporation Street was used there, but the rest was stored by George North at his factory at Piddington. The first Meeting for Worship at 'The Limes' was held on 29th December 1929. It must have been a cheerless occasion but better things were to come, in the shape of a property a short way from 'The Limes' along the London Road. The story is well told by the report of the MM Finance and Property Committee dated 10th March 1931:

New Meeting House at High Wycombe

The new Meeting House is at last an accomplished fact. At the date of the last report we were still looking unsuccessfully for suitable premises, and were considering the possible purchase of Bardon House in Easton Street in order to erect a new Meeting House behind it. Local Friends however discovered that a beautiful little 18th Century house was shortly coming into the market, on the London Road facing the open space known as The Rye. This was Fairwood Cottage, for thirty years the residence of Mr. Fred Skull the well known dealer in antiques. The house was found to be quite adaptable to our requirements and the price finally agreed at £1,750 freehold.

Mr. Skull had already purchased a quantity of old panelling and beams from our former Meeting House in Crendon Lane (now demolished) and fitted them into his new home in Bassetsbury Manor. He was particularly glad that his old home should pass into our hands.

Sam North was appointed architect for the necessary alterations which are estimated to cost £750 in all. These with the legal expenses and outgoings bring up the total cost to approximately £2,550. This figure exceeds the sum realised by the old Meeting House by about £260 and this deficit is being met out of general funds of the MM.

The Meeting House premises are on the ground floor and the upper floor has been converted into a very satisfactory self-contained flat which it is proposed to let at £52 p.a.

It is very satisfactory to report that the whole project has been carried through without recourse to borrowing and the Meeting House opens its career entirely free from debt .....

In addition to the property we have also taken over the tenancy of a small garden plot opposite the Meeting House adjoining the river – at a rental of 10/- p.a. payable to the Corporation. This preserves the open view and safeguards the little garden from possible deterioration. (By the end of the year the Committee decided to relinquish this tenancy.)

The temporary accommodation at 'The Limes' has been terminated.

Those who wrote the report apparently did not think it appropriate to mention the request made by the PM that Mr. Skull should 'leave the cut bushes representing birds as they form such a charming adjunct to the property'.

A small committee of Davina Watkins (then Clerk of the PM), Jane North and Malcolm Sparkes (Clerk of the MM) had had responsibility for decoration and furnishing. Special attention had been given to seating; locally made wheelback chairs were purchased, and also 10 small rush-seated chairs, with two armchairs of similar design, were ordered from George North, at 20s per chair for the small and 30s for the arm. A number of other chairs formerly used by the Meeting were thus made redundant and disposed of at 2s.6d each -

20 to Chalfont St. Giles Rural Council
30 to Jordans Village Hall
 2 to Katherine Parker
 2 to George Small

The forms used at Corporation Street came to the new room. A new table was made by George North to match the elders bench which had been with the Meeting since the Crendon Lane days and had a place of honour in the new Meeting Room. A noticeboard was designed by Sam North. A new piano was purchased for £35, less allowance made of £3 for the old one.

The first Meeting for Worship was held in the new premises on 15th February 1931, and they were officially opened on Saturday 28th March by Neave Brayshaw. According to the *Free Press* the opening was preceded by an address outside the Meeting House from Katherine Parker, and followed by one inside from Harry T. Silcock. After that and an interval for tea at 5.30 there was a 'soiree', music, games, supper and folk dancing. One wonders what quality of Meeting for Worship there was the next morning, but there is no doubt that there was in Wycombe in 1931 a vigorous and enthusiastic group of Quakers, now with premises very sensitively adapted to be suitable for Quaker worship and activities. As it was to turn out, vigour, enthusiasm and much use of the premises were all to be key features in the challenging years that followed.

HIGH WYCOMBE
Crendon Lane

23 Members. 19 Attenders.

† KATHERINE PARKER (MRS.), (Clerk to P.M.), *The Shrubbery, Amersham Hill, High Wycombe.*
JANE NORTH (MRS.) (Assistant Clerk). *Arosa, Amersham Hill, High Wycombe.*

Meeting for Worship: 1st-day, at 11 a.m.
Fellowship Meeting: 6.30 p.m first 1st-day in the month (October to May).
Men's Adult School: 1, White Hart Street—1st-day at 9 a.m.
Women's Adult School: Y.W.C.A. Hut, Victoria Road—5th day at 7 p.m.
Railway Station: High Wycombe (G.C. & G.W.R. Joint), ¾ mile.
Market: 6th-day

(*) ANDERTON, WILLIAM, *Priory Avenue*
(a) BACKHOUSE, BASIL HENRY, *The Pines, Penn,* [*Bucks.*
BACKHOUSE, DOROTHY EMILIE
(c)   Emilia Margaret
(c)   Edward
(t) DAVIS (Miss), ANNE ALICE, *Rayners, Penn*
(*) BOOTH (MRS.), IDA, *Hyden, Upper Hughenden* [*Road*

LUTON AND LEIGHTON M.M.   37

(*) DAIRY (MRS.), KATE, *Hyden, Upper Hughenden Road* [*Aylesbury*
DUNN (MISS), LILY, *Berncliffe, King's Road,*
(*) ELLERY, EDMUND JOHN, *Littledene, Loudwater*
ELLERY, FLORENCE GERTRUDE
(*) GARNER, OSBORN WILLIAM, 284, *Slater Street*
(*) GUNSTON, AMY M., 4, *Hillside View, Upper* [*Hughenden Road*
(*) HALLESEY, DANIEL, 135, *Hughenden Road*
(*) HOUGHTON (MISS), CLARIBEL, letters to 39, [*Leamington Road Villas, Bayswater, W.*
HOUGHTON, WALTER
HUNT, SIMEON, 4, *Totteridge Lane,* [*Totteridge*
HUNT, JANE
NORTH, GEORGE EDWIN, *Arosa, Amersham Hill*
(o) NORTH, JANE
(c)   Edward Samuel Lithgow
(c)   Hector
(c)   Peter
(c)   Ida Lithgow
(ac) PARKER (MRS.), KATHERINE, *The Shrubbery,* [*Amersham Hill*
(*) PARKER, CHARLES A.
    Elizabeth
(*) PERRY (MRS.), ALICE, *Wharf Side Cottages,* [*Stratford Road, Buckingham*

HIGH WYCOMBE.   38

PLUMRIDGE, CLARA, *Hill View, Boundary* [*Road, Woburn Green*
(*) PURVIS, ELIZABETH, *Haughmond, Amersham* [*Hill*
ROSE, WALTER, *Aston Road, Huddenham,* [*Bucks.*
ROSE, MARY LOUISA
    Elsie Mary, at Sidcot School
    Marjorie Doris
(*) SALTER, WILLIAM E., *Golf View, Flackwell* [*Heath, Loudwater*
(*) SALTER, JENNIE
(c)   Gladys
(c)   Winifred
(*) SMALL, GEORGE ALFRED, 28, *Roberts Road*
(*) STEEVENS (MISS), SARAH, 30, *Crendon Lane*
(t) TROOD (MRS.), ANNIE ELIZABETH, 169, *London* [*Road*
(t)   Stella Margaret Edith
WATKINS (MRS.), DAVISA, *Ridgmont,* [*Rectory Avenue*
(c)   Ivy
(c)   Beryl
(c)   Enid
WATTS, HARRY, *Baden Villa, Roberts Road*
WATTS, ANNIE
WHITLOW, ARTHUR, *Daybrook, Ranelagh* [*Road, Bracknell, Berks.*

Appendix — High Wycombe Meeting 1922.

CHAPTER 10

A Multitude of Causes

IN 1931, WHEN Quakers were enthusiastically settling into their new Meeting House in London Road, the town of High Wycombe was also going through a very busy period. The furniture trade was still engaged in meeting demands from new municipal buildings, schools and libraries that were just opening. (Wycombe library opened in 1932). But by 1932 the mass unemployment that had struck many areas of the country was affecting Wycombe, and there were 2,000 people without jobs. L.J. Mayes relates that 'a Council of Social Service (CSS) was formed and relief measures started to help feed and clothe the families of the workers', and behind the new Public Library the derelict buildings, formerly Wheelers' brewery, were turned into the Malthouse Club for the unemployed. It was to stay open for seven years.[1] Robert Day represented Friends on the CSS, and the Meeting provided the club with four benches from the Meeting House.

Quakers had been active centrally on unemployment since 1926, investigating conditions and organising relief work, notably in South Wales:[2] and had also established the Allotment Gardens Scheme for England and Wales. In January 1933 Wycombe Meeting founded a local branch of the scheme. The Meeting House was made available on three mornings a week for receiving applications from unemployed people, and in March Walter Houghton reported that 180 applications for seeds, tools and seed potatoes had been received. By the end of the year 220 men had been assisted. The Meeting met all the working expenses of the scheme.

Fifty years later one historian, describing the policies of the National Government of 1935 with reference to unemployment and the 'depressed areas', wrote that 'little was done to remedy the causes. There were local philanthropic gestures by the Quakers and other idealists'.[3] This somewhat dismissive statement deserves a response, for without it much that was undertaken by Wycombe Friends in the

1930s and 1940s could be misunderstood. The truth is that in tackling social or international problems it will often be found that Quakers, generally at national level, have done their best to tackle causes, within the limits of the knowledge and facilities available at the time. But when these have failed, they have seen 'local philanthropic gestures' as a natural expression of their concern. This was the case over unemployment, and will be seen to be so over other matters referred to later in this chapter.

An immediate example of this situation is seen in Friends' interest in reconciliation with Germany, which went back to the first world war. In 1930 the Friends International Centre was established in Berlin to try to foster mutual understanding and peacemaking, and Friends such as Corder Catchpool gave much of their lives to this cause. He was the British representative at the Centre in Germany, and from him came reports in 1933 of the first organised assaults on Jews, and fears that war with Germany might arise again.(4) Members in Wycombe were to be affected by this situation in two particular respects.

First were considerations of what the Quaker peace testimony was to mean for yet another generation. Walter Houghton represented the Meeting at a gathering with others to consider the formation of a branch of the British Anti-War Movement, but he reported that Friends could not wholly identify themselves with it for the movement 'condoned certain kinds of war'. In 1935 the High Wycombe Peace Council was granted occasional use of the Meeting House for its meetings, and Jane North and Catherine Biggs represented the Meeting on it. And in 1936, at the instance of Maurice Evans, a weekly study circle on the pacifist position was established.

The subjects for speakers at Fellowship Meetings in the autumn of 1937 indicate the discussions going on amongst Friends and attenders: they were 'Christianity and Peace'; 'Is Christianity out of date?'; 'An equivalent of war'; and 'What is Christianity?'. Elders reported to Monthly Meeting that attendances at evening meetings had grown, to about 30, and that 'outsiders' appreciated the addresses. There is no doubt that throughout the country the Quaker peace testimony became better known during the three or four years preceding the war, and male membership of the Society grew: and this growth was reflected in the membership of Wycombe Meeting.

The second respect in which the situation in Germany closely affected Friends in Wycombe was that of refugees. Meeting for Sufferings, as the executive body of Friends centrally, minuted its grave concern in December 1938 at the persecution of Jews and non-Aryans.

In January 1939 Wycombe PM appointed William Bond, Maurice Evans and Stanley Tennant to consider what practical steps could be taken locally to help those who had fled to Britain. One result, for example, was the payment of regular contributions over two years towards the costs of a place for a refugee boy at Woodside, a special school in Loudwater with which Jordans PM was associated, and whose committee William Bond then joined. The boy concerned went to America after two years.

A little later an International Club for Refugees held its meetings on Thursday evenings at the Meeting House. Albert Branch, who lived with his wife Olive in the flat at the Meeting House for a period from 1938, was particularly concerned with this, though records do not indicate how the club was founded. It was later reported that there was an average attendance of 25-30, from nine different nationalities. The club offered English lessons of one hour each week; assistance in writing letters in English, to those not sufficiently advanced in their knowledge of the language; help in finding work, and in finding cheap lodgings in the locality for those who had found it; and advice in such matters as National Insurance.

Already it will be seen how important to the activities of the Meeting the Meeting House had proved to be since its opening in 1931. When it opened the flat was let at a market rent, not necessarily to a member of the Society. But in November 1933 MM considered the matter and minuted as follows: '... it has been shown that the MM has received considerable financial benefit in the past as owners of the property. It is suggested that the activities and influence of the Meeting are hampered by the present arrangement and the desire is expressed that the MM should provide for a resident member of the Society, living in the flat, and at a reduced rental with an honorarium to promote extension work'. There is no record as to when this was arranged or who was involved, until 1938 when Albert and Olive Branch became wardens. They removed and went to Surrey in 1944.

In September 1940 Walter Houghton died, at the age of 67. *The Friend* paid tribute to his 'long and loyal service' to the Meeting.

> 'Although ordinarily silent in Meeting, when he did speak it was with great weight and earnestness and a ruthless criticism of wrongdoing. He was an enthusiastic advocate of the education being given by the Society of Friends to its young people and by his will leaves funds for the endowment of a 'Claribel Houghton Trust' for bursaries to be given within the compass of Jordans Monthly

Meeting to the children of Friends at Friends' Schools. Claribel Houghton, his sister, was herself a teacher and a convinced Friend.

Walter Houghton, who was a pacifist, went through life with an uncompromising rectitude which occasionally imperilled his high position in the businesses with which he was associated. He sometimes saw his principles triumph over the evils he was fighting, though in at least two instances he felt compelled to resign.

Late in life he embraced poverty for a period and lived on a fixed minimum, which was modified only when ill-health demanded it as a measure of safety.

Retiring and studious by nature, he delighted in music and the arts and had a wide knowledge of literature.'[5]

The Meeting lost another of its founder members of 1914 when George North left the district in 1942. He lived on for another forty years, dying at the age of 102.

War brought compulsory military service for men, but allowed for 'conscientious objection' to be a cause for exemption after the Conscientious Objectors (COs) concerned had been interviewed by a tribunal. This could allow total exemption, but more usually made any exemption subject to certain conditions such as specified alternative service. Early in 1940 two members of staff of High Wycombe Town Council registered as COs, but before a tribunal had considered the applications the Council resolved to dismiss any employees who did so. Shortly afterwards the County Council decided to do the same. The Ministers Fraternal, the Fellowship of Reconciliation and Wycombe Meeting all wrote letters of protest at this extraordinary example of local authorities taking the law into their own hands, but to no avail.

At the end of the war the Council was obliged, by the Reinstatement under Civilian Employment Act 1944, to take back all employees whether COs or not: they agreed to do so but only for the minimum period of one year required by the law.

As the war went on several men associated with the Meeting registered as COs. In August 1940 Ronald Forward, an audit assistant, and Peter North, a chartered quantity surveyor, were registered conditionally on their doing full-time agricultural or similar work. In 1941 Albert Branch was registered, on condition that he did land or social service. And in January 1942 it was reported to MM that Kenneth Hellowell, a solicitor aged 31, who had been attending High Wycombe Meeting for two years, and joined the Royal Air Force, was in military custody at Redcar; by April he had served a short term of imprisonment at Durham, for refusing to obey military orders, and was awaiting an appeal tribunal as a CO. He came before the Northern Appellate Tribunal and accepted their decision that he should do land work.

In 1940 the MM appointed a 'Watching Committee' for COs, on which the PM was represented. In 1942 it was decided to replace this with local committees, and Ethel Sterry, Amy Gunston and Catherine Biggs were appointed in Wycombe. In 1941 the Meeting House was made available on two or three evenings each week so that COs working in the district in the Christian Pacifist Forestry and Land Units could meet socially. As these activities imply, though minutes do not mention it, Wycombe Friends, like many Meetings up and down the country, must also have been giving much unofficial moral and social support to COs within their boundaries.

At the end of the war the Meeting began to see something of Seebohm Rowntree, who had moved from York to North Dean, near High Wycombe, in 1937, presumably with later retirement in mind. Though a Quaker, active locally in York, he was better known outside the Society than within it. At the age of 26, when the family firm of Rowntrees Cocoa Works became a limited liability company in 1897, he was a member of the first Board of Directors; and in 1923 he succeeded his father as Chairman, retiring in 1941. He made his name as a sociologist when he published a massive study of poverty in York in 1901. In the first war Lloyd George appointed him Director of the newly-established Welfare Department at the Ministry of Munitions, – Lloyd George called it 'a strange irony, but no small compensation, that the making of weapons of destruction should afford the occasion to humanise industry'. In 1917 he became a member of the Reconstruction Committee preparing for post-war recovery. In the second war he was an adviser to William (later Lord) Beveridge when he was writing the famous Beveridge Report.

When his wife Lydia died in September 1944 after a protracted illness he considered this private tragedy a spur to take on more public tasks, and he moved to a flat in Hughenden Manor in 1946. To the thirty books or pamphlets he had written by that date he added two more with co-author G.R. Lavers.[6] He started coming regularly to Meeting, contributing in ministry and participating in business meetings. He spoke at a public meeting arranged by Friends, on 'the state of the country', when 50 people were present and discussion was reported to have been 'very vigorous'. He became a patron of the theatre in Wycombe (retiring as a director in September 1954) until he found that 'even sitting in the front row of the stalls and using my hearing aid, I cannot hear what takes place on the stage'. He died that same year.

The war officially ended, in Europe on 8th May and in Japan on 15th August, 1945. But much misery remained, and Friends had already become involved in 'philanthropic' work which would extend well into the 'peace'. In October 1944 the Preparative Meeting had been told by Maurice Evans of his concern for the well-being of Italian prisoners of war in High Wycombe.

In this concern Maurice Evans had many precedents in Quaker history. As Lawrence Darton has written:

'The Aliens Section's work for prisoners of war in this country was no new departure for Friends, for not only had they undertaken such work during the first World War, but their interest in war prisoners can be traced back to the eighteenth century. In assisting the German, Italian and other prisoners in the second World War, the Society found exceptional opportunities for a service of reconciliation. This service was seen, first, as one for individuals irrespective of nationality, for fellow human beings in need of friendship and help. In addition, the treatment of prisoners of war was seen as part of a relationship between the people of two different countries with important implications for the future. For Friends did not lose sight of the fact that, when the fighting was over, there could be no lasting peace without co-operation between victors and vanquished.'[7]

When Germany surrendered there were nearly 200,000 prisoners in this country. Friends worked closely with the International Red Cross and the International YMCA, and were able to appoint a number of welfare visitors to POW camps, and also to provide books, musical instruments, and tools and materials for handicrafts, for prisoners. The latter formed part of a large educational programme organised and encouraged by the YMCA. 'After the Armistice' wrote Lawrence Darton, 'the very much greater freedom with which permits to visit the camps were granted and the contact which became possible with prisoners outside the camps, meant that many hundreds, perhaps thousands, of Friends were able in one way or another to play a vital part in the work.'

This, therefore, was the background to the concern of Maurice Evans in 1944. The Meeting gave him their support and made the Meeting House available for social activities. A youth club was formed, attended by seventeen young Italians. By the summer of 1946 nearly all the Italians had been repatriated. But repatriation of Germans was slow and uncertain. The FCRA had written to Wycombe Meeting in January of 1946 asking if it could do anything for German prisoners, and in October it was agreed to help Stanley Stevens, a local Anglican, who had been a member of the Friends Ambulance Unit, who had been appointed an official visitor to German p.o.w. camps in the district. A report written by him on visits to Peterley camp near High Wycombe mentions that the Meeting 'and the local pacifist groups have given a great deal of cooperation in providing things for the camp, and in the short time that has passed, have provided a whole host of gifts, including books, magazines and German papers, paints, notebooks and pencils, a large quantity of apples, essences and flavourings, and decorations for Christmas ....'.

On a lighter note, one wonders how seriously to take the PM minute of 2 February 1947. It reads: 'Stanley Stevens brings requests for womens and other clothing that would serve for the plays these prisoners hope to stage. It is thought that if a list of the cast, with a description of the clothing required and sizes of the men taking part were supplied, then we could loan the required effects as was done with the Italian prisoners of war'. A note later added by the diligent PM Clerk records that 45 German p.o.w.s were given tea at the Meeting House 'prior to their newly formed Concert Party performing at Trinity Congregational Church', and that ' the hall was full and people were turned away'. It is a pity that no record of the performance itself has been found!

It was not until the end of 1948 that repatriation of German prisoners was achieved.

Maurice Evans had also, as far back as 1943, been one of the Meeting's representatives on a local Famine Relief Committee. This was to support the efforts of the National FRC, formed in May 1942 on the initiative of Edith Pye (a Quaker who had campaigned on the same subject in the first World War!) and the Friends Service Council, to press the government to allow food through the Allies' blockade for the relief of overrun countries in Europe suffering from serious food shortage. The government never agreed, and so it was not until May 1946 that the Meeting recorded its willingness to meet the cost of parcels (mainly clothing) being sent to the continent, mainly to returned Italian prisoners. Later a letter was sent to the local press giving the address of the Meeting House as a depot where clothing could be left for Friends Relief Service to send to the continent, and food could be collected for Save Europe Now.

Six months later it was recorded that 5 cwt of clothing and 3 cwt of food, and £50, had been sent. The same month a parcel of food was received from America for needy Friends, with instructions that it was not to be sent abroad! It was decided to use it 'for Meeting House purposes'! The PM minutes of these post-war days make it clear that even by 1947 the need was still urgent to conserve and share scarce resources.

Despite all the practical activity that had been demanding members' time and effort, Elders were able to report to MM in 1947 that the Meeting had grown and that 'new members are proving really helpful'. Most third Sundays there was an evening meeting with a speaker; study circles continued on alternate Tuesday evenings; and a Friday evening meeting had been started with an attendance of 8-12 'to consider the Meeting for Worship and how members can fit themselves for it'. By 1948 the Meeting at last began to feel that the long period of pressure from a multitude of causes, arising from the war and its precursors and its aftermath, was over, and a different era of Quaker involvement had arrived.

NOTES TO CHAPTER 10
1. L.J. Mayes. *The History of the Borough of High Wycombe: from 1880 to the Present Day*, p.68.
2. Note also the significant Swarthmore Lecture of 1933 by Shipley N. Brayshaw, *Unemployment and Plenty*.
3. Kenneth O. Morgan. *The Twentieth Century* in *The Oxford Illustrated History of Great Britain*, p.548.
4. William R. Hughes. *Indomitable Friend: Corder Catchpool 1883-1952*.
5. *The Friend*, November 8, 1940.
6. *English Life and Leisure, a Social Study*, and *Poverty and the Welfare State. A Third Social Survey of York dealing only with economic questions*. Both published in 1951.
7. Lawrence Darton. *Friends Committee for Refugees and Aliens 1933-1950*, p.135.

CHAPTER 11

Quaker Citizenship

'Remember your responsibilities as a citizen for the conduct of local, national and international affairs. Do not shrink from the time and effort your involvement may demand'.[1]

THE PERIOD 1945-51 had been one of national austerity. Indeed rationing for food, clothing, petrol and many domestic commodities survived until 1954. But, as Kenneth O. Morgan relates, 'for all that, most working people, the vast majority of the population, viewed the years since 1945 as much the best that had been generally known since the late-Victorian heyday. Wages rose to 30 per cent above their 1938 level. There were higher living standards, guaranteed employment, more satisfying environmental and educational facilities. In a world, too, where popular sport such as football, cricket, and also the cinema and the dance hall, were readily accessible, the leisure aspects of the good life were catered for as well'.[2]

By 1951 the population of Wycombe had grown to 40,000: and there were fifty members of the Meeting.

Eric Hobsbawm writes of the period 1914 to the aftermath of the Second World War as the 'Age of Catastrophe', which was followed by 'a Golden Age for 25-30 years after that, ending in the early 1970s'. It was 'the age of the automobile; of mass travel; of a technological earthquake transforming everyday life bringing, for example, the transistor, the freezer, t.v., tapes, domestic electronics'.[3]

Hobsbawm however goes on to qualify his enthusiasm for the 'Golden Age' with his references to the gloom which all those who were adults at the time will remember, the dark shadows of the 'Cold War'. The roots of this were in the convictions of the USA and Western nations of Europe that the Soviet Union had intentions of promoting communism by military aggression, out of which in 1949 grew the

North Atlantic Treaty Organisation (NATO), which would become the basis of western opposition to Soviet military policy for the rest of the century. But it was the events of 1954 which made the climate of the Cold War. In that year the US had tested a hydrogen bomb, a relatively small one but still 600 times the power of the atom bomb dropped on Hiroshima in 1945. The British prime minister, Winston Churchill, thought that in future international conferences, 'only the powers with nuclear weapons would occupy the top table' and told the cabinet that Britain would build the bomb. The view from Moscow was of an alliance almost entirely circling the Soviet Union and armed with nuclear weapons, and in 1955 the Soviet Union and seven Eastern European nations ratified the Warsaw Treaty. Two power blocs, each with nuclear weapons, faced each other in Europe.[4] The political climate became one of constant friction between them, and fears of war – or, more likely, of obliteration – amongst their peoples.

Friends were hugely concerned at the situation, and were not slow to express their views. In 1955 Meeting for Sufferings minuted:

'We in Great Britain have decided to make hydrogen bombs. If a major war breaks out the temptation to use them will be very great. We are warned by our scientists that their use will involve not only the most terrible suffering now, but unknown consequences for succeeding generations who will pay the penalty for our sin. We believe that no one has the right to use these weapons in his defence or to ask another person to use them on his behalf. To rely on the possession of nuclear weapons as a deterrent is faithless; to use them is a sin'.[5]

Friends in Wycombe raised questions about the government's decision with candidates at the general election of 1955, and in 1956 unsuccessful attempts were made to get a statement of Quaker views published in the *Free Press*. But they felt that local involvement should go further than this, and in December 1957 the Meeting began to discuss a book by a retired naval commander, Stephen King-Hall, entitled *Defence in the Nuclear Age*, which put forward proposals for non-violent resistance in the face of an armed occupation of our country. A summary of his proposals which was prepared by the Meeting at the time reads as follows:

'The writer points out that war is the expression of a conflict of ideas. In the present cold war we are trying to defend our Western way of life, which is based on the idea that the individual is the most important unit in Society, against attack by the contrary idea that the individual exists for, and is subordinate to the State.

Although ideas are best attacked by other ideas and cannot be destroyed by force, we in this country are basing our defence on military force and are relying on the threat of retaliation with nuclear weapons as our only safeguard against major aggression. The efficacy of this 'great deterrent' is a matter of complete speculation, with the grave disadvantage that if we have guessed wrong, the penalty is the destruction of the nation. The writer comes to the conclusion that there is a prima facie case for abandoning this foundation for our defence and pleads that the best minds in the country should be brought together to consider the question.

'He goes on to examine the consequences of unilateral renunciation of the making, stocking and using of the H-bomb which, he points out, necessarily involves the abandonment of nuclear tactical weapons and of conventional forces for use in a major war. As a result the USA would probably withdraw from Europe and leave us without military defence against attack or occupation. He feels however that even occupation would be a lesser evil than the use of the H-bomb and the conversion of the country into a smoking radioactive charnel house. The alternative to NATO might be a Western Treaty organisation of countries practising non-violence and acting generously in the international field. Even if occupation were the result, we need not be defeated but it would be necessary if possible to plan in advance for such occupation on a wide scale and involving the whole population.'

The Meeting supported the proposals and in 1958 decided to commend them to the Yearly Meeting Peace Committee, suggesting that a group of 'eminent and well concerned Friends should consider where the Society might stand if the King-Hall proposal for a commission was accepted'. It also decided to organise public meetings on the technique of non-violence, and to arrange a study group on the subject.

The Peace Committee appointed a group of its own, but six months later reported that it had made little progress. To take the matter forward the Meeting decided to take it to Meeting for Sufferings. Quaker practice requires that to do so a Meeting must first get endorsement from Monthly -and in those days also Quarterly- Meeting. This was done remarkably quickly, and "Sufferings" considered it in March 1959. Under pressure, in June three members of the Peace Committee met Wycombe members and 'a useful discussion took place'. But by the end of the year it was clear that the Committee could not decide on any action to recommend to Meeting for Sufferings, and Wycombe submitted an article to the weekly journal, *The Friend*, which agreed to publish this and a series of five or six articles to follow it, written by other contributors.

The discussion was also broadened in other ways. Three representatives of the national Direct Action Committee against Nuclear War met a representative of the Meeting, and when their Committee became the Non-Violent Defence Group a representative of the PM attended it. Wycombe Friends were invited by Friends across the country to send speakers to various meetings, including one in Leeds where, it was reported, there were 300 present.

All this was a stimulating exercise, involving a considerable number of the local Meeting, and giving them much work to do, over a period of five years. Its processes provide a typical example of the working of what Friends call "a concern", though it was unusual in that from the beginning it was a *corporate* concern, as opposed to one initiated by an individual. It was however disappointing in its end results. Jordans MM obtained reports from its constituent meetings in December 1960 and minuted:

> 'Although members of some of our Meetings are active in practical peacemaking within their areas, it seems apparent from these reports and from our discussion that Friends are not united in their opinion as to the way the Society should meet the challenge of the nuclear deterrent ... We realise, however, that the Society does not appear to have sufficiently positive answer to the mounting dilemma, and it is hoped that further serious consideration of the method and implications of non-violent action may be instituted by the Society, possibly through the medium of Woodbrooke.'

Wycombe Friends had to accept that the Society did not have the positive answer they wished to see.

Was the whole exercise a waste of time? Local Friends never thought so, but a Quaker concern springs from an impulse which has to be obeyed, and having followed it as far as they can those involved are content – even if disappointed – to leave it there. There may be some comfort in a historian's comment on the Campaign for Nuclear Disarmament (CND), which was formed in 1958. It had a more limited objective than that of Wycombe Friends, but

> 'CND members continued to campaign for what they saw as their logical point of view, even though they believed that the government would ignore them no matter how hard they campaigned. CND's campaign was however, a constant reminder to the public,

and particularly to government, that there was a protest movement based entirely on ethical grounds'.[6]

A number of Friends in Wycombe joined CND and supported the local group.

Joining with others to promote causes or provide services, rather than to do so as a Meeting, became the norm. In 1968, in another connection, the Meeting noted:

> 'It is not agreed that a common mind and service and witness can and should develop over large areas of the secular field e.g. education, welfare and social service. It is felt that in this kind of field, the Church as such may not have the professional expertise required, and that the individual Christian would do better to get into the various organisations alongside other concerned people, who may not be Christian, there to work and witness'.

Wycombe Friends joined various movements, quite often becoming secretaries or chairmen for periods of years. They participated as individuals, not as representatives of the Meeting. This means that there is no full record of what the movements were, though Amnesty, United Nations Association, Wycombe Society, World Development Movement, are found at times in the minutes. Official support was always given to the local Council of Churches and Christian Aid Week.

Various organisations looked for support from Friends in the use of the Meeting House. Examples at this time were Alcoholics Anonymous, Marriage Guidance, Adult Literacy Schemes, Hard of Hearing, Blind Association: and overnight on Good Friday 1965 the premises were occupied by 40 participants on the CND march from Naphill (Bomber Command)!

During the 1950s and 1960s over a million people from India, Pakistan, West Africa and the West Indies migrated to Britain. Over 1,000 had settled in Wycombe by 1960, and the Mayor called a meeting to discuss the situations of overcrowding and exploitation in which many of them found themselves. As a result, the High Wycombe Overseas Consultative Council was formed, on which David Griffith, a member of the Meeting, played a leading part. The Council found that shortage of low cost housing was the cause of the overcrowding, and this led to exorbitant rents being charged for such accommodation as was available. Although Wycombe was regarded as a 'boom town' in that there was no unemployment, there was a shortage of jobs for unskilled workers, and unemployment began rising steadily. By 1961 race prejudice was also evident.

As a contribution to meeting the housing situation the Consultative Council formed the Wycombe Friendship Housing Association. It opened seven houses, each divided to provide at least two homes. Friends agreed to form a house committee for one of these, and did so from 1969 to 1978.

In addition to Meeting for Worship every Sunday morning a programme of evening meetings with a speaker was arranged every year at least during the winter, continuously up to 1958. These were partly for members, providing information and stimulus from Friends with particular knowledge or experience; and also for other local people, who did not come to worship but were learning about Quakerism or interested in the subjects covered by the lectures. By 1958 numbers attending were dwindling, no doubt partly caused by the spread of television, so regular evening meetings were discontinued and have never been revived.

Just as the age of the public meeting was over, so church attendance was declining, as competing demands from other activities on Sundays grew. Wycombe Meeting was bound to be affected, and some of the remaining chapter is devoted to an assessment of its future.

NOTES TO CHAPTER 11
1. *Quaker Faith and Practice*, para 1.02, 34.
2. Kenneth O. Morgan. *The Twentieth Century* in *The Oxford Illustrated History of Great Britain*, p.569.
3. Eric Hobsbawm. *Age of Extremes. The Short Twentieth Century 1914-1991*.
4. Christopher Lee. *This Sceptred Isle. Twentieth Century.*
5. *Quaker Faith and Practice*, para 24.41.
6. Christopher Lee. Op. cit.

CHAPTER 12

Quaker Community

IN THE 1960s numbers attending Meeting for Worship averaged 20 and were not growing, but numbers of children increased. In 1962 the children's class was held every other week, with an average attendance of five. But younger children arrived and in 1966 there were five children in a senior class and seven in a junior. It was therefore decided to reduce the size of the warden's flat, and make two rooms upstairs available for use at any time for children's or other purposes. By 1968 there was a "third-Sunday creche" for four "pre-school" children, and in 1970 the creche was provided every Sunday except the first in the month. The ground floor of the Meeting House in those days had no room suitable for any classes, and for a time some of the children went to a Friend's house nearby.

For some years this arrangement was acceptable, but taking the children upstairs, where they were over the Meeting for Worship, was not ideal; the kitchen, which was a tiny space next to the Meeting Room, was proving inadequate; and the toilet facilities were unattractive if not primitive. It was therefore of great benefit to the Meeting when a legacy from one of its members, Nora Wickens, in 1980 enabled it to extend the premises to provide a good-sized committee/children's room, a large kitchen, and new toilets, all served by what the architect's plans appropriately named the 'chat lobby'.

During the 1970s all PMs within the MM including Wycombe were finding that 'Pastoral Care and Religious Training of Children and Young People' was proving difficult because the number of children in any one Meeting was small and the age range large. To some extent the difficulty was being redressed in that, as Overseers and Elders recognised, many teenagers stayed away from Meeting for a time 'in order to assert their growing independence', and this had to be accepted, though meetings of young Friends on a MM basis for a while provided a substitute. Monthly Meeting camp was also recommended for those of 11 and upwards – 'as well as being great fun it provides a unique opportunity to get to know other children in the Monthly Meeting and to take part in discussions, both formal and informal'. (As the years went on camp changed, to become as it is today, one for families, valuable in itself but not focussed only on older children).

So far as younger children were concerned, by 1974 other Meetings were giving much less teaching of the kind normal 10-15 years earlier, e.g. bible stories and teaching based on courses of lesson notes obtained from Friends House and elsewhere. The emphasis was instead 'put on activities which the children enjoy'! Wycombe went on a little longer: it reported in 1978 that it had a group of 'about seven 8-10 year olds in our Childrens Meeting, and they have enthusiastically discussed aspects of Quaker testimonies, some of the Advices and Queries, Friends Service Council projects, and heard about the Reformation. Other topics have included our PM, Christian law, and helping others in the third world. The younger group ... have heard their own simple Bible stories, ... with plenty of practical work'. But by 1987 Elders reported that 'children's classes are at a low ebb everywhere', and High Wycombe did not have one. Since then, the class has been revived, but has a struggle to maintain any constancy of attendance, although in 1999 there was a potential of 10 children from 5 families.

When children are born to families attending Wycombe Meeting it is usual for them to be brought into a Meeting for Worship at an agreed time, and to be welcomed by a member chosen to speak for all those present. In due course those attending childrens meetings will, it is hoped, come into adult Meeting for Worship for a short period at the beginning or end as agreed by the PM. It is recognised that there are today real problems in trying to communicate religious experience formally, but, as one report put it, 'by coming to Meeting, the children do become aware that, in Meeting, we seek to make contact with a secret power which we regard as of supreme importance in every aspect of our lives. We should not underestimate the ability of even very young children to enter into the spirit of worship'.

In 1986 the saga of the burial ground came to a conclusion. The last burial there had been in 1913, and it seems that the ground got little attention during the first world war or for some time afterwards. In 1927 Francis Colmer made a sketch of it (Appendix I), which may have pricked the consciences of Friends, for by 1932 it was recorded that the ground had been tidied up in various ways. In 1936 it was decided to suggest to the Council that the ground should be made into a public open space, and MM decided to offer it the land free of charge. It was conveyed to the Council in 1937.

This however was not the end of the story. Although in 1944 fourteen headstones were sent to the town cemetery for safe keeping, in 1947 the indefatigable Katherine Parker, who had started the Meeting in 1914, was again expressing disgust at the state of the ground, to no avail: she died in 1949. In 1964 the Council wrote that it was proposed to develop the land for residential purposes, but the Meeting resisted, considering that to be an inappropriate use for it. The proposal must have stimulated anxiety in the Steevens family, many of whose members had graves there, for A.E. Steevens sought assurance that Quaker ground might be found for the bodies elsewhere if necessary. The PM was able to obtain that assurance from Jordans burial ground in 1965, though the offer was never taken up.

Then in the 1970s the Wycombe Society set its sights on what was dubbed the 'Eastern Desert' of the town, the Saffron Platt area, where development had been inhibited by a proposal for a new road to run parallel to, and north of, the London Road, but which had been cleared of many old properties and left derelict. In 1980 the *Free Press* gave a full page to the matter. 'Demolition craze leaves old area "torn up by its roots"' was its heading. On the Quaker Burial Ground it quoted the Wycombe Society:

> 'The use of the burial ground for storing empty beer barrels is unsightly and we feel that action should be taken against this flagrant abuse of council property. The use of the Quaker burial ground as a car park is deplorable and could easily be prevented by the District Council. The unauthorised users should be made to use the official car park. If the area could be cleared of beer barrels and cars, the council could then consider it worthwhile to restore the burial ground to its former very agreeable appearance. This Society would be willing to help in this work'.

In 1982 the WDC agreed to 'improve and fence the ground', which meant in practice turning it into a garden for public use, and in 1985 the Meeting was able to record that 'the garden has at last been completed by the local Council, nicely laid out with shrubs, lawns and paths'. And on 19th July 1986 the garden was formally opened, by Council vice-chairman Len Hampton and David Griffith of the Meeting. A historic moment!

Other events before the end of this period were also by way of being 'historical'. The Borough of High Wycombe had as a local government unit been absorbed in 1974 into the much larger Wycombe

District Council, but certain mainly ceremonial functions had been continued and a Mayor is still elected annually. In April 1998 the PM recorded that 'The Mayor of High Wycombe for the year 1st May 1998 to 1st May 1999 has invited Brian Gelsthorpe (a High Wycombe Friend) to be her "chaplain". She has asked us to allow her to bring a procession of town officers and trustees to attend a Meeting for Worship during her year of office'. This was agreed, and the official Civic Service for 1998 took place on 31st May. Twenty seats were reserved for those who came in the procession, and the mace which headed it was placed on the piano during Meeting for Worship. A copy of *Quaker Faith and Practice* was presented to Frances Alexander, the Mayor, to mark the occasion.

It is interesting to think back to the Mayor of 1665, himself the embodiment of the authority of the Borough, who broke up meetings of Quakers and sent some of them to prison. The 20th Century occasion just described seems to have in it some element of poetic justice.

History too on 16-17 September 2000, when at the request of the organisers of 'Heritage Weekend' the Meeting House was open to the public, and information about it and Quakerism was made available. This successful event was followed in 2002 by the completion of a small permanent display of eleven pieces of archive material, which are now mounted and framed, with explanatory captions, on the wall of the Meeting Room and the lobby (Appendix II).

Fascinating though history is in itself, its value must also be in helping us to make our way into the future. In the second half of the 20th century in Britain there have been members who have warned the Society of pitfalls ahead. In her Swarthmore Lecture of 1967 Kathleen Slack analysed her study of seventeen meetings: though membership of the Society was at that time slowly increasing she was anxious about who would be available to carry out the responsibilities of running it. Women were becoming less available to help, mainly because more of them were in employment, and Friends generally seemed to be 'serving more frequently on the committees of other bodies today than their own'; and also giving a wide variety of voluntary service to other than Quaker organisations. The weight of responsibility was falling on Friends of retirement age, who comprised about 25% of the membership. She felt that if these trends continued there would be deterioration in the life of the Society.[1]

Alastair Heron had similar fears but for a different reason. He summarised them in 2001:

'1. During the nineteen-eighties the total adult membership remained constant at just under eighteen thousand, but *during the last decade it has fallen by twelve hundred.*
2. This decline in membership has been caused by a *progressive reduction in the annual number of new members on 'personal application'*, which from a high point of nearly five hundred in the mid-eighties, has fallen steadily during the nineties, and is *now less than three hundred.*

The opposite trend holds for 'Recognised Attenders': just over six thousand in 1981, reaching nine thousand in 1991, still at that level today'.

Alastair Heron went on to say:

'To these facts should be added the reports of local and monthly meetings finding it increasingly difficult to identify seasoned Friends, for service as clerks, elders and overseers, who have not already served for six or more years in one or more of these capacities. Similar difficulties beset nominations committees when seeking suitable Friends for service as appointed representatives on Meeting for Sufferings, and the Representative Councils.

In the light of this weight of evidence, it is time to recognise that *Britain Yearly Meeting is facing an increasingly serious human resources problem.*

The existence of this growing problem is entirely due *to the progressive fall in the numbers of Attenders seeking membership of the Society.* Since new members can come only from our Attenders the future of British Quakers lies in their hands'.[2]

To what extent are these causes for anxiety as described by Kathleen Slack and Alastair Heron found in High Wycombe Meeting? Kathleen Slack's point about women being less available is true, in that more of them are employed full-time and have less voluntary time to offer. Her point about Friends generally giving active support to non-Quaker voluntary organisations is also valid. And more responsibility may indeed be falling on people of retirement age, though there are more of them in Wycombe (about 30% in the Meeting today), and perhaps they are also fitter!

Alastair Heron's anxiety is first about total membership. In Jordans MM the decline in numbers over the past decade in fact more than reflects that of the YM, as it fell from 322 in 1989 to 289 in 2001. But in Wycombe numbers rose slightly, from 46 to 50 over the same period. The numbers of attenders recorded in the MM list for Wycombe was

22 for the year 2000, which is not quite as high a proportion of the membership as in the YM.

In Wycombe, though there *is* difficulty in finding Friends to meet some demands, it is not as acute as it might be because membership is not declining. But the Meeting would certainly like to see more of its attenders joining in membership.

As a passage in *Quaker Faith and Practice* puts it:

'Membership is a way of saying ... that you accept at least the fundamental elements of being a Quaker: the understanding of divine guidance, the manner of corporate worship and the ordering of the meeting's business, the practical expression of inward convictions and the equality of all before God'.[3]

Today a Meeting for Worship in Wycombe comprises an average 20 people, meeting for one hour, in which silence will be broken perhaps by two or three short oral contributions, though occasionally it is completely silent. After it is over, coffee or tea is available, giving those present a chance to meet visitors, to get to know one another better, to exchange news and views, perhaps to discuss personal problems and experiences, or to arrange matters concerning the Meeting's business. More serious opportunity to go into matters of Quaker faith and practice is given in the study group which meets fortnightly on a weekday evening, and is keenly supported by 10-12 members. Meetings for business take place on the first Sunday of each month after Meeting for Worship.

A Quaker Meeting is at its best suitably described as a community, and although Quakers experience the same demands on their time as is common to many people today, those who do maintain a fair constancy of attendance at Meeting for Worship find it a great source of strength and joy.

The Quaker community has now, for all but one short period, existed in High Wycombe for nearly 350 years. This brief history has shown that it has stood tests of much stress and strain, but maintained a consistency of faith and practice. It should have much to contribute in the years to come.

NOTES TO CHAPTER 12
1. Kathleen M. Slack. *Constancy and Change in the Society of Friends.*
2. Alastair Heron. *The Future of British Quakers*, p.5.
3. *Quaker Faith and Practice*, para 11.01.

Appendix I – Burial Ground 1927. Drawing by Francis Colmer.
COURTESY OF BUCKINGHAMSHIRE COUNTY MUSEUM

Appendix II

Archives on display in Meeting House:

1. To the keeper of the gaol at Aylesbury.
   An order dated 1st July 1665 for the imprisonment of ten Quakers.

2. Plan of the Quaker Burial Ground at Saffron Platt.
   A plan listing some 150 graves from about 50 different families.

3. Friends' Meeting House, Crendon Lane.
   Pencil sketch by Francis Colmer, dated 28th August 1924, showing the Meeting House, originally a barn.

4. Interior of Friends' Meeting House, Crendon Lane.
   Pencil sketch by Francis Colmer, dated 1924.

5. Meeting Room in the Crendon Lane Meeting House.
   The screen shown in this print was constructed to separate the men's and women's business meetings.

6. Cottage adjacent to the Crendon Lane Meeting House in 1922.
   A rear view of the cottage that adjoined the Meeting House to the north and was occupied by the caretaker.

7. Crendon Lane in 1910.
   This photograph looks south down Crendon Lane.

8. Meeting Room in Corporation Street.
   This room was used for meetings from 1925 to 1930.

9. Opening Ceremony of Friends' Meeting House in 1931.
   Friends' Meeting House, 25 London Road, and sundial with names of people present.

Index of Personal Names Associated with Wycombe Meeting
(Exclusive of appendices in chapters 8 and 9)

N.B. Where there are two or more persons of identical names, they are distinguished by showing their dates of reference.

ARCHDALE, Anne, 25
Archdale, John, 22, 23, 24
Archdale, Mary, 25

BALL, George, 13, 16
Beale, William, 53
Bellamy, Adey, 39, 40, 41, 42
Bellamy, Judith, 39
Bellamy, Martha, 39
Bevan, Priscilla, 53
Biggs, Catherine, 73, 76
Bond, William, 74
Branch, Albert, 74, 75
Branch, Olive, 74
Brown, Elizabeth, 18

COCK, John, 13, 16

DAY, Arnold Maurice, 61
Day, Cecil Gordon, 61
Day, Robert, 72
Dell, Thomas, 13, 16
Drewett, Beryl, 53

EDMONDS, Anna, 53
Edmonds, Elizabeth, 46, 49, 50, 53
Edmonds, Grizzell, 50, 52, 53, 56
Edmonds, Grizzell Mary, 53
Edmonds, Jane, 53
Edmonds, Priscilla, 53
Edmonds, Rachel, 53

Edmonds, Rebecca, 50, 53
Edmonds, Sara, 53
Edmonds, Samuel (1798), 40
Edmonds, Samuel (1820), 46, 50, 53
Edmonds, Thomas, 40, 46, 48, 50, 53
Edmonds, William G., 43, 50, 53
Endall, Elizabeth, 53
Endall, Samuel, 53
Evans, Maurice, 74, 77, 78

FAGE, Edward, 39
Fage, Mehetabel, 54
Forward, Ronald, 75

GELSTHORPE, Brian, 89
Green, Ann, 50, 54
Green, Joseph, 35
Green, Mary, 36, 46, 54
Green, Susanna, 50, 54
Green, William, 54
Griffith, David, 84, 88
Gunston, Amy, 76
Guy, Samuel, 8, 10, 23

HALLASEY, Daniel, 63
Hargreave, James, 39
Harris, Charles, 20
Hawgood, Ann, 46
Hellowell, Kenneth, 75

Holland, Robert, 54
Houghton, Walter, 62, 72, 73, 74
Hunt, Elizabeth, 54
Hunt, Jane, 62
Hunt, John, 54
Hunt, Mary, 54
Hunt, Simeon, 62
Hunt, William, 54
Huntley, Anna, 50, 52
Huntley, Elizabeth, 47, 54
Huntley, John, 50, 51, 52, 56
Huntley, Richard, 47, 54
Huntley, Sarah Adams, 48, 54
Huntley, William, 43, 47, 48, 54

KEMBALL, Elizabeth, 16
Kemball, John, 16
Kendall, D., 63

LAMLEY, John, 54
Lamley, Samuel, 54
Lamley, Sarah, 54
Lane, Thomas, 10, 14, 16, 17
Line, Ann, 54
Littleboy, John, 13, 16
Lucas, Elizabeth, 46, 49
Lucas, Richard, 43, 46, 49

MEAD, John, 16

NORTH, George, 61, 62, 63, 67, 75
North, J. Lithgow, 63
North, Jane, 62, 66, 73
North, Peter, 75
North, Sam, 67, 69, 70
Noy, Nicholas, 8, 9, 13, 16, 17, 19
Noy, Phillichristi, 9, 16

OLLIFFE, Thomas (1695), 23, 27
Olliffe, Thomas (1712), 27
Orger, George, 39, 40, 46, 54
Orger, Sarah, 54
Orger, Sarah Jnr., 47, 54
Orger, Thomas, 40, 46

PARKER, Katherine, 59, 61, 62, 63, 66, 70, 88
Pattison, Sarah, 54

Philps, Hannah, 54
Philps, Susanna, 54
Polley, Mary Ann, 54

RAUNCE, Frances, 10, 16, 17, 25
Raunce, John, 8, 12, 13, 16, 17, 18, 19, 20, 21
Raunce, Thomas, 17
Robinson, Sarah, 54
Ross, Joseph, 13, 16
Rowntree, Lydia, 76
Rowntree, Seebohm, 76
Russell, Sara, 16

SEXTON, Mary, 22
Sexton, William, 12, 14, 16, 22
Small, George, 62, 67
Spire, Anthony, 8, 16
Steevens, Ann (1665), 16
Steevens, Ann (1820), 54
Steevens, Anna, 50, 54
Steevens, Elizabeth (née Hawgood) (1781), 35
Steevens, Elizabeth (1820), 50, 54
Steevens, Elizabeth (1820), 54
Steevens, Elizabeth (1913), 55, 56
Steevens, Jeremiah, 8, 13, 16, 17, 19, 27
Steevens, Joseph (1664), 13, 16, 18
Steevens, Joseph (1781), 35
Steevens, Mary (1791), 39, 50, 54
Steevens, Mary (1820), 50, 54
Steevens, Mary Jnr. (1820), 54
Steevens, Rebekah, 54
Steevens, Sara, 16, 18
Steevens, Sarah (1820), 54
Steevens, Sarah (1915), 60
Steevens, William, 46, 54, 55
Sterry, Ethel, 76

TENNANT, Stanley, 74
Thurlow, James, 43, 48, 50-51, 54
Thurlow, James Jnr., 51, 54
Thurlow, Lydia, 50, 54
Thurlow, Sarah, 51, 54
Trendall, Lucy, 54
Trendall, Sarah, 46
Trone, Richard, 16, 18

Trone, Samuell, 13, 16

WALDUCK, John, 39, 54
Walduck, Sarah, 54
Watkins, Davina, 62, 63, 69
Watts, Harry, 63
Wells, Henry, 54
Wheeler, Lucy, 54
Wheeler, Mary, 16

Wheeler, Nathaniel, 16
Whitlow, Arthur, 62
Wickens, Nora, 86
Wilkinson, Esther, 42, 48, 54
Wilkinson, John, 42-43, 47, 48, 54
Wilkinson, Martha, 54
Wilkinson, Sarah, 42, 49, 54

YOUNG, Eleanor, 54

Index of Other Personal Names

ALEXANDER, Frances, 89
Aris, Richard, 21

BEVERIDGE, William, 76
Brayshaw, Neave, 60, 70
Brown, Edward, 59

CATCHPOOL, Corder, 73
Colmer, Francis, 31, 87
Cotterell, A.P. I, 63
Cotterell, O.M., 68
Cripps, Charles Alfred (Lord Parmoor), 62
Curtis, Thomas, 12
Curtis, Ann, 12

ELLIS, Marian, 62
Ellwood, Thomas, 10, 12, 14, 17, 18, 21, 22

FOX, George, 4, 9, 12, 18, 19, 20

GEORGE, Lloyd, 76

HAMPTON, Len, 88
Hawks, Helen, 19
Heron, Alastair, 89-90
Holland, P., 63
Huntley, Joseph, 52

INNES, Katherine, 67

KENNEDY, William, 63
King-Hall, Stephen, 81

LAVERS, G.R., 76
Lucas, Benjamin, 46
Lucas, Elizabeth, 46

MARSH, Harold, 63

PARMOOR, Lord (C.A. Cripps), 62
Pye, Edith, 78

RACKHAM, William, 63

SILCOCK, Harry T., 70
Skull, Fred, 68-69
Slack, Kathleen, 89
Smith, Humphrey, 8
Sparkes, Malcolm, 63, 69
Stansfield, Charles, 67
Steevens, A.E., 88
Stevens, Stanley, 78
Story, John, 20

TRITTON, Fred, 67

WAUGH, Jane, 17
Wilkinson, John, 20

ZACHARY, Thomas, 21

General Index

ADEY Bellamy's legacy, 42
archives, display of, 89, 93

BIBLE, Friends and the, 47-49
Burial Ground, HW, 24, 55-56, 87-88
burial grounds, 24
burials, 24, 55-56

CAMPAIGN for Nuclear Disarmament, 83-84
Census of Religious Worship 1851, 51
children's classes, 86-87
Commonwealth (Roundhead), Quaker relations with, 11
conscientious objectors,
  first world war, 61-62
  second world war, 75-76

EDUCATION, local involvement with, 43

FAMINE Relief, 78-79
'Fellowship Meetings', 60, 65, 67, 85
first world war,
  concern about, 60, 65
  conscientious objectors, 61-62
  military service, 61-62
France, war with, 1793-1815,
  rates imposed for, 40-41
  relief work, 41

GREAT War – see first world war

IMPRISONMENT, 12-14, 17, 21-22, 27
itinerant Friends, 9, 17, 41-42, 42

JORDANS Monthly Meeting, 67-68

LIBRARY, at Meeting House, 42, 61
Local government, 41

MARRIAGES, procedure, 19
'Marrying-out', 35, 46, 57
Meeting House,
  Corporation Street, 67, 68
  Crendon Lane,
    acquisition of, 23, 25
    after 1870, 55, 66-67
    alterations to, 42
    details of, 26-27, 29-32
  Easton Street, 68
  London Road/Stuart Road,
    alterations to, 68-69, 86
    civic service at, 88-89
    lettings, 84
Membership
  local estimate of numbers 1770, 34
  list, 1665, 16
    1820, 53-54
    1915, 64
    1922, 71
  service to the Meeting, 89-91
Monthly Meetings
  established by George Fox, 18
  women's, 20

OVERSEAS Consultative Council, 84

PARLIAMENT, elections,
  1698, 25
  1832, 43-44
Particular Meetings (PMs), 18, 33
peace testimony, 12, 73
  non-violence, 81-83
  nuclear weapons, 80-81
persecution, 21-22
personal circumstances, 37 –
  see also Adey Bellamy's legacy
personal conduct, concern about, 27, 34-36, 37-38
plague, 17-18
prisoners of war, 77-78

'QUIETISM', 27

READING and Warborough MM, 52
refugees, 73-74

SECOND world war,
  conscientious objectors, 75-76
separatism of John Raunce,
  20-21
social circumstances of Quakers, 14-15, 36

TITHES, non-payment of, 11,
  37-38, 39-40, 57
travelling ministers – see
  itinerant Friends

UNEMPLOYMENT, 72-73

Upperside Monthly Meeting, 18-20,
  33-35, 41-42
Upperside & Leighton MM, 52

WARDENSHIP at Meeting House, 74
Wooburn, Meeting at, 22
Worship, 8, 27, 58
Wycombe Friendship Housing
  Assn., 85
Wycombe Meeting,
  Allowed, 59
  closure of, 52
  Preparative Meeting approved,
    62